Practical
Pre-School

GW00691600

The ELGs in Practice
Practice

Revised and updated September 2000

By Gay Wilkinson

Contents

2	Introduction
8-10	Personal, Social and Emotional Development
11-14	Communication, Language and Literacy
15-17	Mathematical Development
18-21	Knowledge and Understanding of the World (Science, Design and Technology and Information Technology)
21-24	Knowledge and Understanding of the World (History)
25-27	Knowledge and Understanding of the World (Geography)
28-31	Physical Development
32-35	Creative Development
36-37	Assessment
39	Assessment sheet (photocopiable page)

Many elements of pages 8-35 of this material have been published previously in Issues 1-8 of *Practical Pre-School*. However, the book has been fully revised to take account of the Early Learning Goals and the *Curriculum Guidance for the Foundation Stage*.

Illustrated by Cathy Hughes

Published by Step Forward Publishing Limited, The Coach House, Cross Road, Milverton, Leamington Spa CV32 5PB
Tel: 01926 420046
Published in Great Britain © Step Forward Publishing Limited 2000

The ELGs in Practice   ISBN   1-902438-39-6

Introduction

The Government announced its intention of revising the Desirable Learning Outcomes within the paper, *Excellence in Schools*. Following consultation by the Qualifications and Curriculum Authority (QCA), the Government published the booklet *Early Learning Goals* in October 1999. In September 2000, these goals replaced the age-related Desirable Learning Outcomes (DLOs). All settings registered with their local Early Years Development Partnership to receive nursery grant funding and schools with nursery and reception provision are now inspected according to the Early Learning Goals (ELGs). In addition, private and voluntary settings registered with their Partnership will continue to be required to:

● have regard to the DfEE's Code of Practice for special educational needs;

● make information available to parents about their educational programme and other matters;

'For children to have rich and stimulating experiences, the learning environment should be well planned and well organised. It provides the structure for teaching within which children explore, experiment, plan and make decisions for themselves, thus enabling them to learn, develop and make good progress.'

● agree to have their educational provision inspected regularly by the Office for Standards in Education (Ofsted) and make the inspection report and the action plan available to parents.

When they published the Early Learning Goals the Government also announced its intention of issuing more detailed curriculum planning guidance to support practitioners in implementing the new goals. In May 2000 the Government published the document *Curriculum Guidance for the Foundation Stage* and this was circulated to all providers. The Government has also published and circulated *A Training Support Framework for the Foundation Stage*, a multi-media package designed to support all practitioners in using the QCA/DfEE *Curriculum Guidance* effectively.

'The curriculum should be carefully structured, planned and organised. The structure should contain three strands: provision for the different starting points of children (building on what they already know and can do), experiences that match the different levels of need and 'planned and purposeful' activities that give real opportunities for teaching and learning both indoors and outside.'

The Early Learning Goals

Whilst there is some difference in the wording of the goals compared to the Desirable Outcomes practitioners will recognise that in general there is little difference between the two. For example, in Personal and Social Development the DLOs talked about children being 'eager to explore new learning' whilst the Early Learning Goals talk about children continuing 'to be interested, excited and motivated to learn'. Overall the changes are to do with vocabulary rather than content. Whilst the goals themselves remain broadly similar to the Desirable Outcomes they have been clarified and itemised for easier reading and identification. In some cases the goals have been written so that they clearly take account of the specified age range represented in the booklet. In the cases of Communication, Language and Literacy and Mathematical Development, the goals have been amended to take account of the National Literacy and Numeracy Strategies so that the more flexible learning that occurs in these curriculum areas in the Foundation Stage will feed into the Literacy and Numeracy Hours that children will experience in the National Curriculum.

The Early Learning Goals are presented in booklet form. As well as the goals there are a number of other sections on related aspects that provide a clear context for the learning goals for the Foundation Stage. These aspects include principles for early years education and common features of good practice. The booklet also includes a range of other helpful material including:

● General aims for the Foundation Stage

● Specific aims relating to each area of experience

● Play as a key learning process in the early years

- The diverse needs of children

- Special educational needs and disabilities

- English as an additional language

- Parents as partners.

Whilst the goals themselves will clearly receive particular attention, it is important that practitioners read and reflect on all the sections in the booklet to help them in developing high-quality experiences in their setting.

The six areas of learning originally identified in the Desirable Outcomes document are retained in that of the Early Learning Goals. However, 'Communication' has been added to Language and Literacy and 'Emotional' has been added to Personal and Social Development. As before, each area has its own set of specific outcomes that most children are expected to achieve.

However, there is a significant difference between the expected age of achievement stated for the Desirable Outcomes and that given for the Early Learning Goals. The expectation for the DLOs was that most children could be expected to achieve them by the age of five when children are required to begin statutory schooling. The expectation for the ELGs is that most children can be expected to achieve them by the end of the reception year at which time some of the children in any year group will only just be five whilst others may well be almost six.

The most significant development within

the publication of the Early Learning Goals is the recognition that the early years are a distinctive and important phase of children's development in their own right. Accordingly the Government has now established a Foundation Stage that precedes Key Stage 1 of the National Curriculum. This stage begins when children reach the age of three and finishes at the end of the year during which children become five. This final year of the Foundation Stage is commonly referred to as the reception year since most children are admitted into the reception class of a primary school at some point during this year depending upon the admission patterns adopted by individual schools. The goals set out what is expected for most children by the end of this Foundation Stage and lead into the National Curriculum that all children are

required to follow from Year 1 of their statutory schooling. The Early Learning Goals, within the context of the Foundation Stage, are therefore an important measure in promoting curriculum continuity between the different settings that children may attend in the early years as well as with statutory schooling. They also provide a sound basis for all children's future learning within and beyond school.

It is the responsibility of the staff in a registered setting to design, plan and implement a curriculum that takes account of the Early Learning Goals within a context that recognises the

needs of all the children for whom they have responsibility. It is this curriculum that is inspected by Ofsted and it is on the findings of the inspection that successful registration with the LEA depends. Therefore to become registered with an LEA and be eligible to receive the nursery grant funding, settings must take account of the goals to ensure that their provision supports and extends children's knowledge, skills and confidence, and helps them to overcome any disadvantage.

The booklet clearly defines those factors which should ensure that all early years educational provision is of high quality by setting out a statement of principles for early years education. It takes account of both research about teaching and learning in the early years and what practitioners said during the consultation. These principles are drawn from, and are evident in, those settings where good and effective practice is in place.

The principles underpinning high-quality provision

- The experiences and activities provided should build on what children know and can already do. They should enable children to feel that they are learners and therefore to want to go on learning. This will protect them from experiencing early failure.

- No child should be excluded or disadvantaged because of race, culture, religion, home language, family background, special educational needs, disability, gender or ability.

- The curriculum should be carefully structured, planned and organised. The structure should contain three strands: provision for the different starting points of children (building on what they already know and can do), experiences that match the different levels of need and 'planned and purposeful' activities that give real opportunities for teaching and learning both indoors and outside.

- Children learn through play and in other ways and the planned curriculum should take account of this. Children do not make a distinction between play and work and neither should practitioners when talking about or describing activities with the children.

- Opportunities for children to be involved in both activities planned by adults and those they have planned and initiated for themselves.

- Opportunities for children to work for regular sustained periods of time without constant interruption and time to complete both adult-set and self-initiated activities.

- Opportunities for children to work in small and large groups.

- Adults who spend time with the children listening to their ideas, talking to them and taking a real interest in what they are trying to achieve - 'practitioners must be able to observe and respond appropriately to children, informed by a knowledge of how children learn and develop'. Effective education needs practitioners who understand that children develop rapidly.

- Adults who understand that teaching and learning is a partnership between themselves, the children and their parents. To ensure that all children feel secure and valued, practitioners must establish and maintain positive relationships with parents - 'children, parents and practitioners must work together in an atmosphere of mutual respect'.

Curriculum Guidance for the Foundation Stage

The guidance is presented in ring-binder format. This not only makes it easy to use but also provides practitioners with the opportunity to add other related materials relevant to their setting, as they require. As with the Early Learning Goals, the QCA consulted with early years practitioners and experts as well as working closely with the National Literacy and Numeracy Strategies and Ofsted in developing the guidance to promote high-quality provision and appropriate continuity between the Foundation Stage and Key Stage 1 of the National Curriculum. The guidance is the core reference document for the Foundation Stage. It is designed to help practitioners in developing a common language to describe everything they do with, and provide for, children and most importantly to assist them in developing and providing high-quality experiences in the Foundation Stage. Such experiences will ensure that children are given the best possible start in life and will help them to develop those qualities they will need for later effective learning and development.

There is a close match between the content of the guidance document and the Early Learning Goals booklet. Thus

there is a section that describes the Foundation Stage, a section describing the aims for this phase and one that addresses the issue of partnership with parents. As with the Early Learning Goals booklet there are also summative sections that address the following issues:

Meeting the diverse needs of children

This section focuses on the different experiences, knowledge, skills and interests that each child brings to an early childhood setting, whether at three, four or five, that will affect their ability to learn. Some will have experienced living in a richly cosmopolitan society whilst others will have only experienced living in a community that reflects their own culture, religion and language. Some children may have personal experience of living with someone with a physical or learning disability, some may be coming to terms with a particular need of their own, others may not have experienced these sorts of difference until joining an early years setting for the first time. Some children will already have a rich understanding of a wide range of stories whilst others may have little experience of books. Practitioners are reminded of their need to be aware of current legislation relating to diversity and that in developing and implementing their curriculum they should plan to meet the needs of all the children within their care so that they can make the best possible progress.

Children with special educational needs and disabilities

The importance of working closely with parents as well as with staff from other agencies is emphasised. The section also includes a range of practical and helpful suggestions relating to supporting children with special educational needs.

Children with English as an additional language

The importance of valuing linguistic diversity and planning for and providing opportunities for children to develop and use their home language in their play and learning is noted. The document also highlights the need for those children who are learning English as an additional language to have practical and relevant experiences that

give meaningful opportunities for talking and interacting with others, both children and adults. A range of helpful suggestions completes this section.

Of particular significance to practitioners is that the key principles, identified in the *Early Learning Goals* booklet as underpinning a high-quality curriculum, are repeated (although with slightly different wording and in a different order) at the beginning of the guidance document. Furthermore the guidance states that these important characteristics of the curriculum form the basis from which all the elements contained in the document have been developed. To help practitioners understand these principles fully there is a detailed section on putting the principles into practice. The text is presented in a helpful format that assists in the easy identification of the features of good practice with further exemplification provided by examples of the principles in action. A statement of what practitioners will need to do, followed by bulleted points of the common features of good practice that result from the principles being implemented, are listed in black down the left-hand side of the page. The examples of how these principles have been put into practice in a range of different settings (including a reception class, playgroup, pre-school and a childminder) are in coloured boxes alongside the relevant good features points.

The curriculum can be described in two ways:

● The things that children get to know and understand; the received or learned curriculum - Learning

● The activities and experiences thought out for children and the work done with them by adults; the planned and offered curriculum - Teaching

The main focus of an inspection will be upon these two aspects of the curriculum; the quality of children's learning and how teaching, and those aspects of the setting that support teaching, are contributing to high-quality learning.

The guidance provides a detailed description of the main features of learning and teaching. As with the section on the key principles the text is presented in a format that will help

practitioners to identify information quickly and with ease. Key features of effective learning and teaching are itemised down the left-hand side of each page. Additional comments and examples that show these features in practice are placed alongside each statement in highlighted boxes.

Learning
This section is about the received or learned curriculum. It is about everything that children do, see, hear and feel, both planned and unplanned, within a setting. The features of effective learning noted relate directly to the key principles and are as follows:

● Children initiating activities that promote learning and enable them to learn from each other;

● Children learning through movement and all their senses;

● Children having time to explore ideas and interests in depth;

● Children feeling secure, which helps them to become confident;

● Children learning in different ways and at different rates;

● Children making links in their learning;

● Creative and imaginative play activities that promote the development and use of language.

Teaching
This section is about the planned and offered curriculum. It is about

everything that practitioners do within a setting. As with the features of effective learning the features of effective teaching relate directly to the key principles and are as follows:

● Working in partnership with parents, because parents continue to have a prime teaching role with their children;

● Promoting children's learning through planned experiences and activities that are challenging but achievable;

● Practitioners who model a range of positive behaviours;

● Using language that is rich and using correct grammar. Recognising that what is said and how the practitioner speaks is the main way of teaching new vocabulary and helping children to develop linguistic structures for thinking;

● Using conversation and carefully framed, open-ended questions because this is crucial in developing children's knowledge;

● Direct teaching of skills and knowledge;

● Children teaching each other;

● Interacting with and supporting children in a way that positively affects the attitudes to learning that children develop;

● Planning the indoor and outdoor environment carefully to provide a positive context for teaching and learning;

- Skilful and well-planned observation of children;

- Assessing children's development and progress to serve several purposes. Assessment opportunities may be identified in planning or arise spontaneously;

- Working with parents, who are vital partners in the planning and assessment process;

- Identifying the next step in children's learning to plan how to help children make progress;

- Using assessment to evaluate the quality of provision and practitioners' training needs.

There are also additional sections on teaching and learning, with examples of the features in practice, included in those parts of the document that deal with each of the six areas of learning. These highlight those things that practitioners need to pay particular attention to in that area of learning. Whilst there are similarities between both the general and the specific features related to learning and teaching, those in the areas of learning are particularly related to each of the specific areas. Thus practitioners acting as positive role models to support Personal, Social and Emotional Development could include sharing decision-making with children, whilst in Communication, Language and Literacy

they could include talking to children about past events so that they can hear and learn how words change when the past rather than the present tense is used. These sections on learning and teaching provide essential and supportive reading for all practitioners.

Practitioners should note that the section on learning and teaching is followed directly by a summative section on play. This re-emphasises the importance of recognising that play in a secure environment with effective adult support is a key way in which young children make sense of the world and use new learning in a way that is both enjoyable and challenging. Play helps children to think at a high level. In play children can take risks, think imaginatively, build up ideas and concepts, learn and practise skills and make mistakes. They can play alone, alongside or with other children and talk to others as they explore, investigate and solve problems. They can express their fears as well as their joys, learn how to control their impulses and understand the need for rules. Practitioners are reminded of their need to support children's learning by planning and resourcing a challenging environment, by providing planned play activity both indoors and outdoors, by supporting and extending children's spontaneous play and by extending and developing children's language and communication in their play.

The greatest part of the guidance

document is given to the six areas of learning. To assist in planning, each section dealing with an area of learning sets out those features that practitioners need to give particular attention to, features of effective teaching and learning and the stepping stones for each area. However, practitioners should remember that in the Foundation Stage much of children's learning occurs through play and talk and that many of the activities they plan for children will reflect more than one of the areas of learning and therefore a range of stepping stones may be evident during any one activity. Accordingly practitioners will need to become familiar with all the stepping stones so that they can recognise them in children's activity.

Stepping stones

Practitioners should not feel daunted by this new element included in the guidance nor feel that these will represent an additional pressure upon the curriculum. Careful reading will reassure practitioners that they are often commonly accepted markers of children's development and progress with which they are already familiar. As such, their inclusion as stepping stones should serve to re-affirm the importance of what practitioners already know and help them to understand the significance of this knowledge so that they can use it more effectively in their work with young children.

The stepping stones are a series of learning goals in the Foundation Stage that lead towards achievement of the Early Learning Goals - the final stepping stones. They embody the key principles set out in both the *ELGs* booklet and the guidance. Each area of learning has its own set of stepping stones and the number of stepping stones varies between and within the areas of learning. In some cases several ELGs within an area of learning are grouped together and share a set of stepping stones, sometimes one ELG stands alone with its own set of stepping stones. Thus in Communication, Language and Literacy the two Early Learning Goals 'Use language to imagine and recreate roles and experiences' and 'Use talk to organise, sequence and clarify thinking, ideas, feelings and events' (grouped together as goals for language for thinking) share three stepping stones whilst 'Use a pencil and hold it effectively to form recognisable letters...' (goals for handwriting) is on its own with six stepping stones. Not all the Early Learning Goals have stepping stones for each of the age bands within the Foundation Stage, depending upon the nature of the goals themselves. For example, the two ELGs grouped together as 'language for thinking' (see above) only have stepping stones for five- and six-year-olds. Practitioners will find the ELG groupings, where they occur, useful in managing and planning the curriculum.

The stepping stones and their accompanying features are presented in tabular form to support easy reading. They act as a detailed description of each area of learning and are designed to act as significant signposts of children's progress. Their purpose is to help practitioners understand what learning that will lead towards achievement of the Early Learning Goals actually looks like for young children throughout the Foundation Stage. They show the knowledge, skills, understanding and attitudes that children need to learn and develop during this stage in order to achieve the Early Learning Goals and therefore act as a basis when practitioners are planning the curriculum for the children in their setting.

The stepping stones are not age related. However, to help practitioners use them they are presented in a hierarchical order wherever possible, with those stepping stones, or goals, that generally describe three-year-olds placed in a yellow band, those that generally describe four-year-olds in a blue band, those that generally describe five-year-olds in a green band, with the Early Learning Goals themselves in a grey band.

It is important when using the stepping stones to remember that all children are uniquely different - the principle of diversity. The quality of the experiences they have had before the Foundation Stage varies enormously. Some children will come from homes where they have

few opportunities to handle and learn about books; some may have never had the opportunity to paint and stick or explore a variety of different materials but have already learned a great deal about books and be familiar with a range of stories; some may be anxious about making a mess or getting things wrong. Children's progress in achieving the various stepping stones will reflect this diversity. They may achieve some of the later stepping stones in one area of learning whilst still developing confidence in some of the earlier ones, they may achieve some stepping stones quickly whilst others take much longer. Therefore, by the end of the Foundation Stage some children will still be working towards some or all of the Early Learning Goals, some may have achieved them, whilst others may have exceeded them. If all children are to make the best possible progress there is no substitute for practitioners knowing where children are in their learning and development so that the next step that is planned is appropriately challenging but achievable. This can only be achieved through working closely with parents and through regular and careful observation and assessment. To assist practitioners in assessing progress the stepping stones are accompanied by examples of children in action. These put the stepping stones into familiar contexts so that practitioners will have an understanding of what learning looks like for each stepping stone. These

examples will help practitioners to identify when either individuals or groups of children in their setting have achieved the knowledge, skills, understanding and attitudes inherent in each stepping stone.

Since the curriculum is totally dependent upon the practitioners - what is planned and offered - each stepping stone is also accompanied by some ideas of what the practitioner needs to do to support and consolidate the children's learning. However these ideas are not intended to be definitive. Practitioners will need to draw upon their understanding of the interests and knowledge of their children, as well as their more general experience in working with young children, as they plan further experiences and activities that will support the children's learning and development.

The Training Support Framework

The importance of training and time for reflection on practice for all early years practitioners is recognised by the publication of the *Training Support Framework* alongside that of the *Curriculum Guidance*. These training materials focus upon the essential characteristics (summed up by the principles in both the *Early Learning Goals* booklet and in the guidance) that underlie a high-quality Foundation Stage curriculum and provide all practitioners with a valuable opportunity to consider their own principles and practice. These materials are designed to help less experienced practitioners think about and take on new ideas as well as providing more experienced practitioners with opportunities to examine, reflect on and review their practice. Practitioners will undoubtedly want to continue to discuss aspects of their own provision in the light of some or all of the various issues discussed in both the *ELGs* booklet and the guidance.

Personal, Social and Emotional Development

'Successful personal, social and emotional development is critical for very young children in all aspects of their lives and gives them the best opportunity for success in all other areas of learning. It is crucial that settings provide the experiences and support to enable children to develop a positive sense of themselves.'

The Early Learning Goals and their stepping stones

There are no significant differences between these goals and the DLOs despite the addition of 'emotional' to the title of the ELGs. This is because emotional development was explicitly included in the Desirable Outcomes themselves although not noted in the title.

There are 14 Early Learning Goals for this area of learning. These are divided into six categories. Practitioners will find this categorisation useful both when planning the curriculum and when making assessments of children's progress. The goals are as follows:

Early Learning Goals for dispositions and attitudes
● Continue to be interested, excited and motivated to learn

● Be confident to try new activities, initiate new ideas and speak in a familiar group

● Maintain attention, concentrate and sit quietly when appropriate

11 stepping stones including the above ELGs

Early Learning Goals for self-confidence and self-esteem
● Respond to significant experiences, showing a range of feelings when appropriate

● Have a developing awareness of their own needs, views and feelings and be sensitive to the needs, views and feelings of others

● Have a developing respect for their own cultures and beliefs and those of other people

11 stepping stones including the above ELGs

Early Learning Goals for making relationships
● Form good relationships with adults and peers

● Work as part of a group or class, taking turns and sharing fairly, understanding that there needs to be agreed values and codes of behaviour for groups of people, including adults and children, to work together harmoniously

7 stepping stones including the above ELGs

Early Learning Goals for behaviour and self-control
● Understand what is right, what is wrong, and why

● Consider the consequences of their words and actions for themselves and others

6 stepping stones including the above ELGs

Early Learning Goals for self-care
● Dress and undress independently and manage their own personal hygiene

● Select and use activities and resources independently

6 stepping stones including the above ELGs

Early Learning Goals for sense of community
● Understand that people have different needs, views, cultures and beliefs that need to be treated with respect

● Understand that they can expect others to treat their needs, views, cultures and beliefs with respect

6 stepping stones including the above ELGs

Achievement of these stepping stones, including the Early Learning Goals, will occur across the Foundation Stage curriculum as well as in specifically planned activities that have a particular focus relating to an aspect of this area of learning.

Beginning any new experience arouses a mixture of feelings - excitement, curiosity and anxiety - in adults as well as children. Adults can draw on other similar experiences to help them cope with these feelings but young children do not have such a reservoir to tap into. Moving from

the familiar into the unknown, even when everyone is doing their best to be welcoming and kind can make a child suddenly feel as though they no longer know how to do everyday things and they lose confidence in themselves.

Whether they are three, four or five they will need time to work out for themselves what this new environment is about, what the routines are, how all the people behave in it, what you do with the equipment, resources and materials (some of which may be unfamiliar) and what the adults in charge expect. As they do this they will need adults who are supportive and recognise how they are feeling. They may need an adult to show them how to use some unfamiliar equipment before they can try it out for themselves. They may need to see an adult playing with unfamiliar resources so that they can learn how to use them by themselves. They may need an adult to help them to join another child or small group by modelling how one might ask if they can join in. They may need to be reminded about routines. They may simply need some time to stand and watch other children playing without being urged into an activity. It is important to remember that young children learn by watching and this is particularly so in the first days of attending a new setting.

To help children in these early days it can be helpful to talk to parents. Parents can alert practitioners to particular characteristics that their child has, for example it might be that they worry about getting things wrong, get anxious when they get their hands messy or dirty, or are used to doing something in a particular way. They can also share their child's special interests with practitioners. Knowing about children through shared information that is built on through careful observation will mean that practitioners can give the children the best possible support when they start so that any dent in their self-confidence is only temporary. In this way practitioners will build up positive and effective relationships with each child that will support their achievement of the personal, social and emotional goals.

It is also important that the early years environment, both inside and outdoors, is carefully planned and organised with predictable routines so that children can feel secure and recognise that they are an important person within it. Only when a young child is secure, happy and confident can a sound basis for learning be established.

(Stepping stones for self-confidence and self-esteem and making relationships)

Differences and similarities

A display which has photographs of each of the children will give powerful messages to each child of how the adults value them as special members of their early years community. You can also use these photographs as a basis for discussion, perhaps at story time, about the differences and the similarities between the children - size, gender, colour of hair, eyes, skin, language and any other elements that the children suggest - and how they feel and think about these. Some children might well be challenged by some of the images they see and the opinions expressed by others. Practitioners will need to have thought about possible issues that might be raised by some children during discussion so that any responses they might make are in keeping with an ethos of mutual tolerance and respect. Practitioners need to remember that if they are to foster a healthy emotional climate children need to be allowed to express different feelings.

The use of story books which celebrate children's achievements regardless of gender, race or other physical differences can be a useful extension to such a discussion as can displays of artefacts representing other cultures which children can look at, handle and speculate about. Play resources - jigsaws, home corner equipment - which show that differences are recognised; the celebration of a variety of festivals and special events; visits from parents with special interests, backgrounds or experiences; visits from people within the community who do particular work regardless of gender will all contribute to the development of tolerance, trust and respect for others within the early years environment. Sensitive adults can also use the planned environment to provide experiences which will enable young children to feel a sense of wonder and awe

at the world around them in their outside play, through the care of pets and through carefully displayed artefacts which will encourage reflection and quiet thought.

(Stepping stones for behaviour and self-control and sense of community)

Experiences at home

At home children know where many things are, especially their own toys, are able to choose and take responsibility for much of their own activity, decide how long they will take to do something, perhaps who they will do things with and will have learned about many things through exploration, investigation and play. They see themselves as and act like learners and those who care for them often reinforce this behaviour. This helps them to feel secure, happy and powerful and they are therefore confident and motivated to continue to carry on finding things out.

They may take part in the day-to-day activities in the home, such as preparing a meal, washing up and putting their toys away. These experiences help the child to feel that they belong in the family and motivate them to make the effort to abide by the family rules.

When first attending a pre-school setting the environment can feel and look very different to the young child. They are unsure of what they can and can't do and this uncertainty can make them feel helpless. Such feelings can damage their sense of self-worth and self-esteem and lessen their motivation to carry on being learners. You should make every effort to ensure that the environment makes sense to the child and allows them to take responsibility both for themselves and some aspects of provision within your setting.

Supporting self-help/autonomy

Resources and equipment should be grouped together by kind, be accessible and labelled so that children can find what they need. Since most young children have limited reading skills, consider how materials and equipment are to be stored and distinguished to support their self-help skills. Open crates of cardboard boxes, plastic sweet bottles or containers (local supermarkets and newsagents can provide a useful and often free supply) all allow children to see what is inside. The use of pieces of equipment to act as labels, such as a jigsaw piece (save that old and incomplete jigsaw!) or a Sticklebrick, or pictures drawn or cut from catalogues is helpful to very young children. Pictorial labels could also be used on storage shelves to help children put containers back where they belong during tidying-up.

There should be plenty of opportunities for children to make choices about what they are going to do, whom they are going to do it with and know that they will have enough time to finish their activity to their satisfaction. Equally they should be encouraged to clear equipment away when they have finished using it so that it is ready for someone else to use. It is important that children see that this is a genuine role that is expected of them by all the adults working in the setting and that they are making a special contribution to the well-being and comfort of everybody. They might need support to undertake this successfully, but they should not see the adults doing it again after they have finished or have it done for them. They may interpret this as meaning that what they had been asked to do was not a serious request.

Equally many daily routines can provide children with the opportunity to take responsibility, such as hanging up their coats and washing and drying their hands. Consider whether some routines could be altered to provide greater opportunities for children to exercise independence. For example, instead of handing out snacks and drinks at snack time could the drinks and food be set out so that children can help themselves when they feel ready for these? A table could be set aside with three or four chairs - perhaps the table could be made attractive with a cloth and a small vase of flowers or ask the children how they would like this area to look - and the children told that this is where snacks are taken. They will quickly learn that they need to have their snacks by a certain time. To ensure that all the children have their snacks they can be asked to put a card with their name or special symbol on into a box when they have finished which can be checked before the end of the session.

Planned activities
Since the way we feel influences everything we do it is important that adults should both plan specific activities for children's emotional development as well as respond positively to spontaneous events within the nursery. Puppets can be useful resources for focusing on feelings with a small group of children.

For example, introduce a sad teddy that tells the children what has made him sad. The puppet teddy can be passed around the group and each child invited to say what else has made the teddy sad that day. A range of puppets, each identified with a different feeling, can be collected and used on different occasions. If these are always available then individual children can also use them when they are finding it hard to cope with difficult feelings.

Structured role-play with small groups can also be helpful. The adult tells a simple story in which conflicting feelings are aroused - for example children refusing to share toys and fighting. The children are then invited to talk about the situation, the feelings of those involved and enact alternative ways of dealing with the situation. In this way they can be helped to develop alternative behavioural strategies and learn how to manage their feelings in an acceptable manner.

(Stepping stones for self-care, self-confidence and self-esteem, and dispositions and attitudes)

Children join a pre-school setting from a variety of home experiences and backgrounds. They have already learned a great deal about how people relate to each other through observing and imitating family members and people they know in their immediate community. They have begun to find ways for themselves of trying out aspects of relationships - their behaviours and their associated body and spoken language - in their imaginative play and with their family. In the new setting, with new adults, they will continue to observe and learn from others and will need opportunities to try out what they are learning both there and at home in their play.

Positive relationships
They need to see the adults around them demonstrating positive relationships with each other, with parents and with themselves. They also need to be provided with a range of group play situations, including those that represent the cultural diversity not only of the community but of society in general, that will allow them to try out how some of these social relationships work. Domestic play and other social play settings, such as the doctor's surgery, a shop, a cafe (there are many others), will allow them to experiment

with relationships and different ways of behaving with others without worrying about getting it wrong. In the play they are always in control and can change or mediate the action if they feel that things are getting out of their control. This sort of social play - trying on different roles - provides them with an opportunity to see what it feels like to be someone else and this in turn allows them to develop a better understanding of how and why people behave as they sometimes do and develop greater tolerance and understanding.

As well as taking on other roles children sometimes also need to play out events within relationships without putting themselves directly in the situation. Small world play such as playing with the dolls' house, small model people, cars or animals often gives children the chance to work through a particular social script that interests them, but at a distance, so that confusing and uncertain feelings can be managed.

There are a wide range of story books that provide children with opportunities to talk about their feelings and those of others and these can be used to support particular situations.

The ability to make friends is particularly important to young children and will play an important role in their later achievement in school, particularly as they become adolescents. Young children may need adults to help them to develop and use appropriate strategies for making and sustaining friendships; adults may need to intervene when situations of disagreement or conflict occur and discuss possible solutions with the children. Positive social behaviour such as sharing, helping and caring for others should be recognised and praised publicly. In this way, all children will begin to establish a set of values that will guide both their present and future lives.

(Stepping stones for making relationships, sense of community, self-care and behaviour and self-control)

> **More detailed support to assist practitioners is provided in the 'Examples of what children do' and 'What does the practitioner need to do?' sections that accompany each of the Foundation Stage goals, including the Early Learning Goals.**

Communication, Language and Literacy

Communication, Language and Literacy

Despite the addition of 'communication' to the title there is no significant difference between the DLOs and the Early Learning Goals except that the different elements have been separated and in some cases expanded to give greater clarity to their meaning. For example, the DLOs referred to children using 'a growing vocabulary' which in the Early Learning Goals becomes 'extend their vocabulary, exploring the meanings and sounds of new words'.

The Early Learning Goals and their stepping stones

The importance of this area of learning is recognised by all practitioners and this is reflected in the number of Early Learning Goals, 20 in all. These are divided into six categories that practitioners will find useful both in planning and in assessing children's progress.

Early Learning Goals for language for communication

● Interact with others, negotiating plans and activities and taking turns in conversation

9 stepping stones including the above ELG

● Enjoy listening to and using spoken and written language, and readily turn to it in their play and learning

● Sustain attentive listening, responding to what they have heard by relevant comments, questions or actions

● Listen with enjoyment, and respond to stories, songs and other music, rhymes and poems and make up their own stories, songs, rhymes and poems

10 stepping stones including the above ELGs

● Extend their vocabulary, exploring the meanings and sounds of new words

7 stepping stones including the above ELG

● Speak clearly and audibly with confidence and control and show awareness of the listener, for example by their use of conventions such as greetings, 'please' and 'thank you'

13 stepping stones including the above ELG

The total of 39 stepping stones in this aspect of Communication, Language and Literacy reflects the importance placed upon language for communication in the Foundation Stage. This includes both non-verbal (using facial

expression, gestures, eye contact, and so on) and verbal communication. Communication and talk is central to children's present and future effective development and learning.

Early Learning Goals for language for thinking
● Use language to imagine and recreate roles and experiences

● Use talk to organise, sequence and clarify thinking, ideas, feelings and events

5 stepping stones including the above ELGs

Early Learning Goals for linking sounds and letters
● Hear and say initial and final sounds in words, and short vowel sounds within words

● Link sounds to letters, naming and sounding the letters of the alphabet

● Use their phonic knowledge to write simple regular words and make phonetically plausible attempts at more complex words

9 stepping stones including the above ELGs

Early Learning Goals for reading
● Explore and experiment with sounds, words and texts

● Retell narratives in the correct sequence, drawing on language patterns of stories

● Read a range of familiar and common words and simple sentences independently

● Know that print carries meaning and, in English, is read from left to right and top to bottom

● Show an understanding of the elements of stories, such as main character, sequence of events, and openings, and how information can be found in non-fiction texts to answer questions about where, who, why and how

17 stepping stones including the above ELGs

Early Learning Goals for writing
● Use their phonic knowledge to write simple regular words and make phonetically plausible attempts at more complex words

● Attempt writing for different purposes, using features of different forms such as lists, stories and instructions

● Write their own names and other things such as labels and captions and begin to form simple sentences, sometimes using punctuation

7 stepping stones including the above ELGs

Early Learning Goals for handwriting
● Use a pencil and hold it effectively to form recognisable letters, most of which are correctly formed

7 stepping stones including the above ELG

Achievement of these stepping stones, including the Early Learning Goals, will occur across the Foundation Stage curriculum as well as in specifically planned activities that have a particular focus relating to an aspect of this area of learning.

One of the most important ways in which children learn about themselves, others and the world about them is through seeing, hearing and using language - talking, listening, reading and writing - and of these talking and listening are the aspects which they master first and which will form the foundation for later reading and writing development.

Meaningful conversation
Parents and carers do not develop a formal structure to teach their children how to construct language - they don't give them lessons to teach them new words. Instead, from the moment of birth they behave as though the child is a language user; they respond to the baby's gestures and sounds as though it were part of a meaningful conversational exchange and talk back.

As the child begins to acquire words and try them out they listen to their efforts, interpret and add other words in order to help them sustain the conversation and continue to do so as the child becomes more competent. Above all, they use talk to accompany the everyday activities of family life and engage the child in conversational partnerships as part of these, providing a context within which the child can construct and extend their understanding of the world.

As a result of being in this rich and supportive language environment, by the age of five most children are sophisticated language users. They have mastered the basic grammatical rules in spoken language, developed a vocabulary that allows them to talk about their immediate world and the people in it, understand that language can be used to make and share meaning and can communicate meaningfully with others. In situations which interest and are of relevance to them they are able to use language to talk about the things they see and hear, express their feelings, ask questions, predict likely events, reflect upon their experiences, past and present, share their ideas and imaginings and take an equal part in conversations.

Awareness of print
As well as becoming confident and competent talkers they have already begun to learn things about literacy - reading and writing. At home and in their community they have seen print being used by parents and other

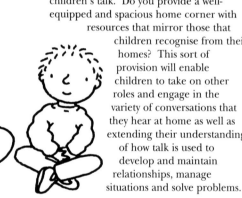

adults as part of real life, for example writing letters, shopping lists and telephone messages and reading recipe instructions or letters. They might even have taken part in some of these events, for example writing their name on birthday cards and adding kisses, and have an understanding that these skills are important for conveying and sharing particular meaning.

They have begun to recognise and remember the shape and pattern made by certain words in their environment and know the sounds associated with each pattern, such as their name, particular shop names, street names, titles of favourite television programmes and story books. It is important to remember, however, that

parents have not set out to teach children to use language and be literate and children do not learn about language and literacy as a subject. The learning that they have acquired is not ordered in any particular way and is closely bound up with all the experiences they have had before they start their early years setting. It has been acquired as part of the social context in which they live - a tool to make sense of the world around them - and they cannot describe what they have learned in subject terms. It is your responsibility to build upon what children have learned informally and through good management, organisation and planning help children to build on what they already know and continue to make sound progress in their language and literacy skills and knowledge.

The early years setting
Children need to be involved in practical, first-hand and interesting activities in order to use language. Do you provide a wide variety of activities, from which children can choose, that will both engage their interest and provide real opportunities for talk? For example, imaginative play is recognised as being particularly valuable for promoting children's talk. Do you provide a well-equipped and spacious home corner with resources that mirror those that children recognise from their homes? This sort of provision will enable children to take on other roles and engage in the variety of conversations that they hear at home as well as extending their understanding of how talk is used to develop and maintain relationships, manage situations and solve problems.

Opportunities to talk
As well as promoting talk through sensitive intervention and participation in children's spontaneous play you can also provide special times when children are encouraged to talk about themselves and events in their lives and learn to listen to what others have to say. Instead of having 'talk time' with all the children together, arrange them into smaller groups, each with an adult. In this way each child has a real opportunity to talk and listen without having long waiting times - very young children sometimes find it difficult to be patient, especially when they have important news to share! Invite parents, grandparents, older children and young people and other people from the community to come in to listen to and talk with the children. The children will benefit

from having more opportunities to engage in conversation with a wider variety of adults. For children for whom English is an additional language it is particularly important that they have opportunities to talk frequently in their first language with other children and adults, as well as being involved in activities which help them to begin to learn English.

Parents and community members who use other languages can be a significant help to you and the children and should be invited in whenever possible.

(Stepping stones for language for communication, language for thinking)

Words and sounds

As children develop their language skills they need to be helped to become more aware of the sounds within words and the similarities and differences between words. This will contribute to later reading and writing success. Regular opportunities to hear and join in with saying or singing nursery rhymes, songs and poetry will both develop their listening skills and strengthen their awareness of sounds. Rhyme is especially important in helping children to recognise the similarities and differences between words. There are a large number of delightful story books written for young children which use rhyme, for example *Each Peach, Pear, Plum* by Janet and Allan Ahlberg (Puffin) and these can be read to them. Once they are familiar with what rhyming means, play a game when reading such stories by encouraging them to guess what word might come next which has both a matching sound and fits in with the sense of the story. Play simple games such as 'I spy' to encourage the children to listen for the sound at the beginning of words - you can adapt other games to do the same thing, for example 'Simon says'. Or adapt 'Kim's game' so that you put out a selection of objects that all have the same initial sound in their names.

Children know that their own names are important and you can use this interest positively to support their understanding of letters and sounds. They often comment about letter

'Communication, language and literacy depend on learning and being competent in a number of key skills, together with having the confidence, opportunity, encouragement, support and disposition to use them.'

features in their own and other children's names, or perhaps see letters in words in a book and recognise similarities - 'I've got one of those'. You need to respond to and use such comments positively. You might consider selecting children to do certain activities such as getting their coats by using initial sounds of names - for example, all the children whose name begins with 'b' - where this is appropriate. Learning to write their own names will certainly provide opportunities to talk about letter features with individual children.

(Stepping stones for linking sounds and letters)

Range of materials

How does your environment reflect the importance of reading and writing in the way the world outside the classroom does? Are there labels attached to particular resources or special displays? Are there signs which give useful information and which will help children make sense of the environment? Do you draw their attention to these by reading them? Do play activities reflect the richness of literacy opportunities that children may experience in their own homes and in their community? Does your home corner encourage them to engage in literacy behaviour by providing opportunities for reading and writing as a real part of their play? Is there a range of different reading materials - magazines, comics, newspapers, cookery books, car maintenance manuals, telephone directories, letters and bills? Is there a range of materials that will support writing - writing paper and envelopes, message pad by the telephone, memo board, shopping list blanks, birthday cards, birthday invitation cards, postcards?

Does other role-play provision developed as part of a theme promote literacy behaviour? For example, a garden centre provided as part of a theme on 'Spring' or

The Very Hungry Caterpillar

'Growth' could have a range of reference books on plants, seed and bulb catalogues, blank order forms and invoices, headed note paper for official letters, blank plant labels and tags, labels denoting different sections of the centre, seed packets and advertising posters.

Planned activities

In addition to these experiences children need to have specific opportunities to take part in activities that will promote reading and writing development. As well as being able to choose to look at and share books in the book corner they should have daily opportunities to hear stories read and told as part of a group activity, in pairs or individually - parents and other adults can be useful for such activities. Rather than gathering a whole group of children together at story time to listen to a story, consider working together with other colleagues or parents and offering two or three stories simultaneously. You will need to provide a brief synopsis of each story and then the children choose which story they want to hear. In this way you will be better able to match the varied reading interests of the children and they will be supported in developing their interest in and enjoyment of reading.

It can be helpful to identify a small number of books that particularly appeal to young children and to use these specifically to develop early reading strategies. By reading and re-reading these with the children (as long as they enjoy them!) they will become familiar with the language used in books (which is very different from spoken language), familiar with how these particular stories work and eventually be able to relate the spoken text with the printed words. Young children love to play at reading and will often select familiar story books to look at, reciting the text from memory. Although they are not reading in the conventional sense they are behaving like readers - an important stage in becoming a reader.

A number of publishers produce books in both a large book format for group activities as well as normal book size. You might consider purchasing some large format story books as well as several copies of the same stories in the normal size so that children can participate in small group activities followed by the opportunity to either have the same book as their friend and 'read' together or 'read' on their own.

As well as the informal writing opportunities provided as part of their play children also need planned opportunities that will encourage them to think about writing. You

could consider developing a writing area in your room which has a range of writing tools available, different papers of good quality, blank books in different forms and other material such as envelopes. The display of models of handwriting or simple alphabet posters in this area would provide those children who are interested with a useful guide when undertaking a writing activity. You will need to stimulate the children's interest in writing - for example, reading the book *The Jolly Postman* might create a positive stimulus for them to want to try out letter writing for themselves. At this stage in their development as writers it is more important that children write for themselves rather than copying from a card or blackboard. However, they do need to be helped to think about how words can be written down and how writing can be organised. A useful activity can be to bring a small group of children together to create a story. In deciding features of the story you can help them to think about how stories work, how using different words can enhance the story and introduce new vocabulary. Once each part of the story has been finally agreed then you can write it down in front of the children so that they can see how writing works. This may also provide you with informal opportunities to talk about and demonstrate different features of print, punctuation, word patterns, letters and letter formation and presentation. At this stage in their development your emphasis should be on promoting their confidence in themselves as writers and helping them acquire the skills of organising their thoughts and ideas so

that they can effectively share them with others.

(Stepping stones for linking sounds and letters, reading, writing and handwriting)

You will need to be aware of what each child is able to do in all the aspects of Communication, Language and Literacy and what new knowledge and skills they might need next in order to make progress and grow in competence and confidence. You will need to observe and assess their language and literacy behaviour regularly, in both their spontaneous play and as they participate in the more structured activities you provide. The judgements you make about each child's progress based upon an analysis of your observations should then be used to help you plan what further opportunities you need to provide which will extend all the children's skills as talkers, listeners, readers and writers.

> **More detailed support to assist practitioners is provided in the 'Examples of what children do' and 'What does the practitioner need to do?' sections that accompany each of the Foundation Stage goals, including the Early Learning Goals.**

Mathematical Development

Mathematical Development

There is little difference between the content of the DLOs and the Early Learning Goals. However, for the purposes of clarity of both reading and understanding some have been reworded and/or expanded. For example, the DLOs referred to 'Use developing mathematical understanding to solve practical problems' which becomes 'Use developing mathematical ideas and methods to solve practical problems'.

There are 13 Early Learning Goals for this area of learning.

The Early Learning Goals and their stepping stones are divided into three categories.

Early Learning Goals for numbers as labels and for counting

- Say and use number names in order in familiar contexts

- Count reliably up to ten everyday objects

- Recognise numerals 1 to 9

- Use developing mathematical ideas and methods to solve practical problems

24 stepping stones including the above ELGs

Early Learning Goals for calculating

- In practical activities and discussion begin to use vocabulary involved in adding and subtracting

- Use language such as 'more' or 'less' to compare two numbers

- Find one more or one less than a number from one to ten

- Begin to relate addition to combining two groups of objects and subtraction to 'taking away'

11 stepping stones including the above ELGs

Early Learning Goals for shape, space and measures

- Use language such as 'greater', 'smaller', 'heavier' or 'lighter' to compare quantities

- Talk about, recognise and recreate simple patterns

- Use language such as 'circle' or 'bigger' to describe the shape and size of solids and flat shapes

- Use everyday words to describe position

- (Use developing mathematical ideas and methods to solve practical problems)

27 stepping stones including the above ELGs

Practitioners should note the emphasis given to talk and practical activity in the ELGs for this area of learning.

Achievement of these stepping stones, including the Early Learning Goals, will occur across the Foundation Stage curriculum as well as in specifically planned activities that have a particular focus relating to an aspect of this area of learning.

Mathematics, like communication, language and literacy, is part of the everyday world. By the age of five young children have already built up a rich experience of mathematical ideas and understanding through exploring and investigating their environment with all their senses.

As very young babies they explored the shapes and space immediately around them, reaching out to touch objects and people near to them. As they began to move around, rolling, crawling and eventually walking, they were able to extend this exploration so that they could interact within different and more complex spaces with a greater variety of objects and materials.

They have picked up and experienced how different shapes feel - the smooth roundness of a ball, the combination of corners, edges and the flat surfaces of a brick. They have tried to put objects together - building a tower with bricks - and have begun to experience how shapes might or might not fit together.

They have arranged and rearranged objects around them and begun to develop an understanding of pattern and the relationships between objects. They will have become aware of the important part that number plays in everyday life as they learn the number of their house, see and recognise numbers on buses or cars, count candles on their birthday cakes, see posters using number symbols in shop windows and buy or watch others buy and pay for a variety of objects during shopping trips. They will have begun to develop a sense of time as they experience everyday routines and recognise recurring weekly, annual and seasonal patterns - days of the week, special days such as their birthday, Christmas, favourite TV programmes.

Each child starts pre-school with their own unique experiences, different abilities and variations in their knowledge and understanding of language to describe their thinking about aspects of mathematics. It is your role - and that of the adults working alongside the children in your setting - to recognise this learning and use it as the starting point for a programme of activities.

When planning how you intend to foster children's continued mathematical development it is important to consider how their early learning has occurred. Much of it will have developed informally in everyday, real-life situations that have been meaningful and interesting; they have been part of the child's continuing process of making sense of his or her world. In organising and planning the mathematical programme it is essential that your environment builds on this early learning and uses those contexts which have already fostered children's interest in exploring mathematical ideas. In this way young children will not only become increasingly mathematically competent, but more importantly, will feel confident and positive that they can succeed as they encounter the challenges that new learning will bring.

Contexts for learning

How does your environment provide recognisable contexts and practical activities which will help young children to use and apply what they have already learned about shape, space, weight, capacity, length, size and number and develop new skills and knowledge?

- Does your home corner have dolls of different sizes with clothing in matched sizes?

- Are there complete sets of crockery and cutlery so that children can match items for a number of place settings at the table?

- Are they allowed to have real liquid in the teapot to pour into the cups?

- Can they make real sandwiches to match the number of children playing or have snack-time fruit or biscuits and share them out as they enact a meal time?

- Are they able to reorganise the furniture within the space and make decisions about fit to meet the needs of their play? Might they be involved in redecorating

and refurbishing the home corner - papering the walls or making new curtains?

- When it's time to clear up are they expected to help by ordering and putting everything away in its proper place?

The well-resourced Foundation Stage environment contains a rich variety of activities and opportunities that will have the potential to stimulate young children's mathematical development. It is your role to recognise the particular mathematical potential of activities and resources and to structure them so that learning does take place.

Shape, space and measures

Children need to be helped to extend their early experiences of shape and pattern and develop a mathematical language that will help them to talk about their ideas and understanding. Activities such as building and making patterns with two-dimensional bricks or tiles of different shapes provide an opportunity to introduce the different names of the shapes and to talk about their similarities and differences. This sort of activity can be either table-top or on the floor depending upon the size of the resource.

Construction play with hollow wooden blocks or large plastic shapes offers the chance to handle and move three-dimensional shapes, learn their names and begin to understand and compare their properties as they build. Painting, printing, modelling and collage further develop children's understanding of shape, space and pattern. All of these experiences need to be freely available each day within your pre-school environment so that children can make mathematical choices within their play. It is useful to have a wide variety of found materials, including containers that are of an irregular shape, as well as regular cylinders, cubes and cuboids, available for children to select from to make models. These will both challenge children in their model making and stimulate them to think and talk about common and different properties.

Throughout all of these practical activities

the children will need the sensitive and knowledgeable intervention and participation of adults as they talk about what they are doing: providing the names of plane and solid shapes - square, circle, cube, sphere; using the language of position - before, next to, under, beside, in front of, top, bottom, edge, corner, opposite; encouraging them to talk about their thinking, drawing attention to specific features and asking open-ended questions which encourage new thinking.

Young children have a genuine interest in play with natural materials. They love to dig and fill containers with sand or soil, adding water to change the way these materials feel and behave - play outside in the garden or inside in the sand tray is always absorbing. They enjoy water play in the same way - pouring, filling and emptying using a variety of resources. They enjoy play at the woodwork bench as they consider how to join pieces of wood together with nails of the right length. As they play they begin to encounter ideas about weight, length, size, density, volume and capacity and make comparisons and judgements. Building horizontally or vertically with blocks or interlocking cubes they will often try to make something 'taller' or 'longer' than themselves and will concentrate for long periods in order to achieve their goal.

Cookery provides further opportunities to understand and make comparisons between the quantity, size and weight of different materials - How does 50 grammes of sugar compare in size to the same weight of butter and flour? Through purposeful and enjoyable activities such as these children will begin to learn the comparative language of measures - full, empty; heavy, light; thick, thin; long, short; tall, small, nearly as, wide, narrow - and begin to make more accurate judgements and refine their understanding.

In all their mathematical experiences exploring shape, space and measures, young children will automatically become involved in using number to help organise their thinking. Indeed, before they start pre-school many children have already learned some of the number names and use counting as part of their play.

(Stepping stones for numbers as labels and for counting, calculating and shape, space and measures)

Number and calculation

It is important to remember that in the real world of the home and family most children will have experienced number being used purposefully, as part of everyday experiences, by the adults around them. How many tins of cat food do we need? How many rolls of wallpaper to paper the kitchen? How many litres of petrol to fill the car? What quantity of material to make the new curtains? Their experience of number is that it is used to help describe concrete experiences where getting the right quantity is important to everyone. It may well be that they have been directly included in some of these experiences. For example, joining in with a parent or carer as a count is made of the number of items to be washed in the washing machine or checking how many tins of dog food are left to calculate how many more are needed. It is essential, therefore, to provide and organise a wide variety of practical activities which children recognise as purposeful. Through their involvement in these activities children will be supported to demonstrate what they already know and new learning opportunities can be planned which will help them acquire new knowledge, learn new vocabulary and practise new skills.

Young children naturally enjoy sorting, ordering and matching materials and objects as part of their play and this will lead them into making counts. In play with the dolls' house, farm, zoo and garage they will sort and classify furniture, model animals and toy cars in a variety of ways - by colour, size, type or kind. They will collect natural objects found outside and arrange them into sets. Play with beads and making necklaces leads

them into eventually creating repeating sequences of colour and/or shape. As they arrange, re-arrange and order all these resources they will increasingly use number names to help describe their activity, make predictions about how many objects they have got and check their guesses by counting. Everyday routines also provide opportunities for children to match and count, for example matching beakers to children, and being responsible (with adult support where necessary) for preparing the biscuits or pieces of apple for snack time will enable them to solve practical problems related to sharing out. What shall we do with the half apple left over?

In all of their activities - sand and water play, role play, small world play, construction, drawing and painting and designing and making - the adults should be observing children's behaviour and, when appropriate, promoting concepts of number and providing associated language - add, minus, take away, more than, less than, the same as, equal to, least, pair, middle, several, enough, first, second, third and one, two, three, and so on.

Planned activities

In addition to these experiences you need to provide specific structured

'Mathematical understanding should be developed through stories, songs, games and imaginative play, so that children enjoy using and experimenting with numbers.'

activities that will promote understanding and use of number concepts. Daily opportunities to hear and participate in number rhymes, songs and stories will develop children's understanding of number value and invariance. In repeating and acting out such rhymes they will be helped to learn and understand the sequence of numbers as well as their names. Teach rhymes, for example 'Five Currant Buns', to help children to count backwards as well as forwards. Pause sometimes in saying the rhyme and ask those children who are secure about the order of numbers what number comes next. You might consider developing your own anthology of number rhymes which the children

particularly like and which offer variety. (The *Practical Pre-School Number Pack* features a selection of popular number rhymes as large colour posters.) This will save you having to look up rhymes in a variety of books and ensure that you offer the children a wide range of rhymes rather than always using the same few.

Equally, when acting out a number rhyme those children who are secure with number order can be encouraged to undertake simple mental computational tasks as part of the activity - How many more will we need to add to make five? If we take two away, how many will we have left? How many all together? Similar activities can be undertaken when they are grouped together for other events, such as preparing to go home. Simple co-operative games that promote counting can be taught and, with the support of adults, played with much enjoyment, for example ludo, snakes and ladders, and various other dice games.

As children demonstrate an interest in mark making to describe what they have been doing they should be encouraged to record their mathematical discoveries, including representation of number value, with their own symbols or by tallying. As they demonstrate awareness of conventional written number forms, and begin to use these spontaneously, they will need to be shown how to form numerals correctly.

(Stepping stones for numbers as labels and for counting and for calculating)

In order to provide appropriately differentiated experiences for children which recognise their different levels of mathematical knowledge and understanding, you will need to develop a sound picture of what they can do. You will need to observe them in all aspects of your provision, both as they engage in spontaneous play and as they take part in the more structured activities you provide, and record their mathematical behaviour (see assessment sheet provided on page 39.) These observational notes should be used to make an assessment of what they know and this should then be used, in discussion with your team, to plan and provide new learning opportunities that will extend their mathematical understanding and competencies.

Knowledge and Understanding of the World

The Early Learning Goals for this area of learning are clarified and expanded to reflect the now established understanding of the importance of children becoming knowledgeable users of information and communication technology. There is also a new addition that reflects the multicultural society in which we live. Otherwise in content they remain largely the same as the DLOs although there is some rewording and expansion to support clarity.

There are 11 Early Learning Goals for this area of learning and these are divided into six categories. The grouping of the Early Learning Goals reflects the different subjects within Knowledge and Understanding of the World.

Early Learning Goals for exploration and investigation
● Investigate objects and materials by using all their senses as appropriate

● Find out about, and identify, some features of living things, objects and events they observe

● Look closely at similarities, differences, patterns and change

● Ask questions about why things happen and how things work

14 stepping stones including the above ELGs

Early Learning Goals for designing and making skills
● Build and construct with a wide range of objects, selecting appropriate resources, and adapting their work where necessary

● Select the tools and techniques they need to shape, assemble and join materials they are using

8 stepping stones including the above ELGs

Early Learning Goals for information and communication technology
● Find out about and identify the uses of everyday technology and use information and communication technology and programmable toys to support their learning

4 stepping stones including the above ELG

Early Learning Goals for a sense of time
● Find out about past and present events in their own lives and in those of their families and other people they know

4 stepping stones including the above ELG

Early Learning Goals for a sense of place
● Observe, find out about and identify features in the place they live and the natural world

● Find out about their environment, and talk about those features they like and dislike

5 stepping stones including the above ELGs

'In this area of learning, children are developing the crucial skills, knowledge and understanding that help them to make sense of the world. This forms the foundation for later work in science, design and technology, history, geography, and information and communication technology (ICT).'

Early Learning Goals for cultures and beliefs
● Begin to know about their own cultures and beliefs and those of other people

4 stepping stones including the above ELG

Achievement of these stepping stones, including the Early Learning Goals, will occur across the Foundation Stage curriculum as well as in specifically planned activities that have a particular focus relating to an aspect of this area of learning.

Science
Science for young children is all about first-hand experience - exploring, investigating and experimenting in order to make sense of the world around them; it is about making comparisons, trying out and testing ideas and considering the nature of what can be seen or what has happened as a result of their actions.

Where young children are encouraged to talk about or plan what they think they want to do and how they might do it, when they observe things closely using all their senses and note and appreciate patterns and relationships, when they use a range of tools to help them in their investigation or if they simply try out their ideas to see what happens, then they will be behaving in a scientific manner and the scientific opportunities within their play and activity will be developed.

To be able to explore and investigate confidently young children need extensive opportunities to handle materials and equipment within their play, sustained periods of time within which they can begin to try to answer some of the problems they will encounter and adults who recognise when it is the right time to intervene.

Your environment needs to be planned and organised so that it stimulates children's natural curiosity about the world around them. Are resources and materials stored at a suitable height? Are they readily accessible? Are similar resources grouped together to make it easier for children to find those that they think they need? Are there displays of materials (for example, a collection of shells, of metal objects, of different fruits) at child height which children can hold, feel, look at closely and even smell or taste that will encourage them to consider similarities and differences and pose questions?

Using displays
A display of shiny objects - mirrors, spoons, silver foil, large sequins - might prompt discussion about reflection and even lead to thinking about how the shape of the reflective surface changes the image. Children could create their own 'shiny' display, bringing objects from home or making a collection of things from within the setting, and so extend the opportunity for further comparison and new questions. Could they sort and classify their displayed objects according to shape, size or other criteria?

You might make a display of cooking ingredients that the children often use in cookery to encourage them to observe similarities and differences. Sugar, salt, cornflour and flour, for example, are all the same colour, but do they smell, taste or even look the same? If you were to mix them with water would they dissolve at the same rate? Ask the children to guess or predict how each ingredient will behave when water is added before mixing and then test to see if they were right. Do remember that children need to do these things for themselves - observation must be personal not copied.

If you are making displays which you want the children to use in this way you will need to consider what sort of guidance or help you will need to give them to ensure their safety.

(*Stepping stones for exploration and investigation*)

The natural world
Where you have access to an outside area or garden, think about how you might develop it to help children think more about living things and the process of life. You might plant shrubs which will attract bees and butterflies for the children to observe or place some logs in one area, the more rotten the better, to encourage insects like woodlice, earwigs and spiders.

Most young children are fascinated by 'creepy-crawlies' and want to catch them. Nature viewers are useful for this. The children can watch the insects through the magnifying lid and see their shape, colour and particular features more easily without harming the insects. How might these insects eat, move, protect themselves? Why are they that colour? Why do they live where they do? For those children who are frightened or tentative about some insects, using a nature viewer helps them to feel safe while allowing them to observe. Once the insect has been carefully looked at then it can be returned to its own habitat.

Birds are natural visitors to gardens and a carefully placed bird table that can be seen easily from a window will enable children to observe them all year round. Put out a variety of foods and observe which birds eat which foods. Keep a list or record in picture form, or by tallying, the birds that are seen.

In their everyday play outside encourage the children to be aware of the weather and seasonal changes. Keep a weather diary and, if you have trees nearby, look at them at different times during the year to observe the changes that are taking place. Make a record of what has been observed with a camera and build up a 'Seasons' book that the children can look at and use to make comparisons. What else could you record in this way that would help the children understand naturally occurring events?

Could you develop an area where the children can plant seeds, care for them and watch them grow? If you plant vegetables as well as flowers then the children can harvest and eat them.

If you don't have an immediate outside area then create one inside! Old sinks make excellent miniature gardens and are deep enough to grow most plants; old tyres can be placed on some heavy-duty plastic, filled with soil or compost and planted up. Seeds can be grown in a variety of containers and even if you do have a garden you may want to grow plants in this way so that the children can observe particular aspects of growth (such as growing bulbs in water to see the root growth) or experiment to see what plants need for healthy growth (not watering some plants or keeping some in the dark).

Keeping pets

Small animals can be kept indoors - dwarf rabbits, guinea pigs, rats, gerbils - and children can help to feed and care for them. Where children are going to handle, move or carry an animal it's a good idea to have a large broad-brimmed ladies' felt hat into which you can put it. The animal can then be carried or held safely and there is no risk of a child being accidentally scratched. This can be particularly supportive for children who are unused to animals and a little nervous. It also prevents the animal being over-handled and demonstrates to the children that we should be thoughtful about the needs of others.

Many providers introduce the idea of life-cycles by bringing in frogspawn so that the children can observe the process of change from egg to tadpole to young frog. Caterpillars, if properly fed and kept, will pupate and eventually become butterflies or moths. The story of *The Very Hungry Caterpillar* would help the children to think about what might happen to their caterpillars and understand the cycle of change. Buy two paperback copies of the book, cut the pictures out and mount them on card - the children can then use these to play out the story and arrange the pictures in the right sequence.

(Stepping stones for exploration and investigation, and a sense of time)

Sand and water

You should always make wet and dry sand and water available. You can try adding different substances to the water - bubble bath, washing-up liquid - so the children can see how the water changes. Let them blow bubbles, observing the shape and colours they see and ask them where else they have seen those colours (a rainbow?). Provide made and natural objects that the children can test to see if they will float or sink. Encourage them to predict how

they think an object will behave and talk about why they think this will be before they try it in the water. Have a range of funnels, containers and tubing so that the children can experiment with the water and begin to find out about its properties. If you're feeling brave, you might let them make waves and observe the effect these have on objects so that they can begin to understand the power and energy of moving water!

Most of the normal range of activities in the pre-school environment will provide children with opportunities to engage in the exploration of scientific ideas. Play with construction materials, for example, allows children to discover the various properties of the materials they use. Use of modular construction kits will allow them to build a variety of models, some of which may have moving parts, such as levers or pulleys, which will help them to consider forces and energy. Play on or with large wheeled toys will add to this experience. Building with large blocks allows them to think about how to make a stable structure and begin to consider how real bricks are joined together.

They can make a variety of sounds in the music corner either with instruments they have made themselves or with commercial instruments, including those from other cultures, so that they can hear and distinguish differences in tone, pitch and volume. In addition to this basic provision you may wish to provide a range of magnets. Children are usually intrigued by their seemingly magical effect on certain

materials! They also really enjoy making simple electrical circuits that allows them to begin to think about electricity. Make a collection of different sized torches for them to use to create both beams of light and shadows. You'll need to create a dark area so the torchlight is effective, perhaps the development of a cave as part of an imaginative play area!

Cookery provides opportunities to make a variety of different foods, including those from other cultures, which will allow them to observe how things can be changed from one state to another (for example creaming butter and sugar or making a batter from flour, milk and eggs), the use of different cooking implements as well as to consider the effect of heat when making something which requires cooking and how the food changes as a result of this process.

(Stepping stones for exploration and investigation, and cultures and beliefs)

Design and technology

Technology is about finding out about and understanding the made world, how it works and how we might influence, modify and change it. When children are using different materials and objects as part of their everyday activity they will be finding out about the different properties of the materials they handle - their flexibility, rigidity, strength, texture, porosity, what they can and can't be used for, their bonding capacity, how they can and can't be joined, the best way to handle them, whether they can be cut, folded, bent, and so on. They will need regular and extensive first-hand experience in order to build up this knowledge. As with science, their understanding needs to be personal, not imagined, told or copied.

Does your home corner have a range of real kitchen tools within it - different shaped whisks, tin openers, timers, sieves and strainers - and are the children shown how to use them safely and given opportunities to use them within their play so that they can observe how they work? Is there a telephone they can use to make calls to real or imaginary friends? Can they build structures with large and small blocks and are they allowed to incorporate other materials, for example building a den with large blocks and using a blanket to make the roof; using a modular kit to construct a crane in the outside sand pit to move the sand from one area to another?

Children need little encouragement to create their own models. Try to provide large tables close to where all the materials children might wish to use are stored. This will allow them to encounter the problems inherent in designing and making something for a particular purpose - which material to select, how suitable it is for the purpose, how they might fit or join things together, which tools to use - and overcome them through trial and error and with helpful support from an adult where appropriate. Designing and making does not always have to be three-dimensional; sewing and collage work also involves design, the consideration of different materials and the use of different joining techniques.

A woodwork bench will allow them to handle tools - hammer, saw, plane, vice - and consider the specific properties of different woods. However, if children are to use real tools, as they should, they must be taught how to use them safely and know the rules for working in that area and there should be continuous supervision of the woodwork bench while it is in use.

As well as building and making things children love to take things apart! Could you build up a collection of artefacts - old clocks, watches, clockwork toys, radios, parts of bicycles - which children can take apart, hypothesise what individual components might do and how the object worked? Ask parents if they have any objects such as these that they would like to donate - you will need to add to your stock regularly! The knowledge children acquire from exploring made artefacts will be incorporated into their own model making and will help them to make sense of the technological world they live in.

The opportunity to use working machines - stop-watches, tape recorders, computers, radios, electronic, battery-powered or clockwork toys, including programmable toys - will further develop their understanding.

Throughout all of these activities it is the adult's role to encourage the children to be reflective about what they are doing, provide new and interesting vocabulary, promote discussion and help them to understand the process of planning, making and reviewing so that they will grow in competency and understanding.

(Stepping stones for designing and making skills, and information and communication technology)

Information and communication technology

Many children will already be familiar with a wide range of programmable equipment such as programmable toys, microwave and conventional ovens, remote controlled televisions and video recorders, automatic washing machines, answering machines, calculators, radios and tape recorders and in some cases may be confident about using them. Many will have access to home computers. It is important that the early years setting builds on all these informal experiences and through well-planned activities helps them to use and extend their knowledge, understanding and skills.

Practical activities such as cooking using both conventional and microwave ovens will provide them with opportunities to think and talk about what is happening and how and why they think this might be. Planning and programming a series of actions for a programmable toy such as a Turtle or Roamer will help them see how things respond to signals and what signals they need to give to get the required effect. Learning how to use a tape recorder and taping themselves, friends or sounds in the environment, using a cassette player and headphones to listen to a taped story or music and knowing how to rewind, pause or

stop it, and pressing the buttons on a calculator will also provide them with opportunities to observe how different objects respond to signals. Many settings now provide children with access to a computer keyboard and printer so that they can learn the basic skills of using these to complete simple programs and begin to understand how they can contribute to their learning.

(Stepping stones for information and communication technology)

Above all, it is the adult's role in planning, managing and organising the learning experiences and supporting that learning through observation of the children and sensitive open-ended questioning - 'I wonder why . . . ?', 'What might happen if . . . ?', 'How do you think this will fit together?', 'What might happen next?' - that will ensure that children's scientific and technological understanding, knowledge and skills are appropriately extended.

History

History is, above all, about people, how they lived and why. Young children are passionately interested in people, in particular themselves and their immediate and extended families. Whilst they are primarily occupied with the present they do have a sense of, and are often fascinated by, the changes that have taken place, both in their own lives and those of others close to them.

They love to look at and talk about photographs of themselves and other members of the family taken in the past. They love to hear stories about when mummy or daddy was little, what it was like and what they did. They ask questions about their own past and want to know what they did at particular times or recall special events that they remember.

They also think about the future; they anticipate and talk about special events that are going to happen to them such as their birthday or going on holiday.

This growing understanding about the sequence of time - yesterday, today, tomorrow; past, present and future - and their ability to both remember and predict events which have personal significance, provides a sound starting point for developing an understanding of history and some of its elements in the early years setting.

Use your community as a resource

In planning and organising your environment you will need to take account of the natural curiosity young children have about their own history and that of others close to them and their innate interest in telling stories. Could you invite someone in to tell the story of some part of his or her own childhood?

Perhaps several children in your group will be having their birthdays around a particular period and are talking about the parties they are going to have. Could you invite a parent or other known adult to come and talk about their memories of birthdays and how they celebrated them?

As Christmas approaches we all know that children's talk is dominated by speculation about presents. Could you invite a grandparent, or other older person in the community, to come and share their memories of Christmas and the sort of presents they wanted and received or some other aspect of their childhood? Since the average life span is now much longer than it used to be there are many people well over 60 in our communities with ample leisure time. Because the last few decades have been subject to immense social and technological progress these people have experienced all sorts of changes as part of their everyday lives. There will be some who can vividly recall a time when there were few cars and most people travelled by bus, tram or steam train; when there were no supermarkets and deliveries of milk and bread were made in a horse-drawn delivery van; when they could go to a shop and buy a pennyworth of sweets. Within this group

there will be some who would love to receive an invitation to share some of their memories with the children and in doing so feel that they can still make a valuable contribution to society.

Preparing visitors

Before any visitor talks to the children it is helpful if you talk to them first so that you can help them select the parts of their life story that you think will engage the children's attention and provide information that matches their current interests. At the same time you might want to discuss with them the size of group they think they will feel most comfortable with and any general rules you have for the children in your setting. In this way you can ensure that the experience is worthwhile and enjoyable both for the children and for themselves.

You might like to consider making tape recordings of these oral history accounts,

providing that your visitors are happy with the idea. After the visit, when you and the children are talking about what they have heard and they are trying to either recall particular information or to re-tell the story, parts of the tape can then be replayed as a reminder.

Such an activity will help them to get events in the right sequence as well as developing their own ability to tell a story, both important skills in thinking about history. If the children represent parts of the story, either pictorially, in words, or both, these can be made into a book with any additional text written by you where appropriate. This can then be placed in the listening area with the tape recording so that the children can revisit the experience whenever they wish.

Familiar objects

Such visits can often arouse children's interests in what familiar objects might have looked like in the past. A visit by a parent or grandparent to talk about the toys they played with as a child could lead to a general interest in old toys. Putting together a display of toys from a particular period alongside a contemporary collection will provide opportunities for the children to consider the differences and similarities between toys then and now and talk about

significant changes. A simple collection of teddy bears would allow them to look for clues that might indicate how old different teddies might be - history is about using evidence. They could then be invited to put three or four into chronological order, starting with the oldest, and to explain what evidence they had used to determine their sequence to the rest of their group or class. It is surprising how many adults keep particular favourite toys from their childhood and many would be willing to loan them to you, especially when they are helped to understand how this will support the children in developing important concepts and skills.

There are many other familiar domestic objects in children's daily lives which intrigue them, most of which have changed over a period of time.

Handling artefacts

Themes or interests such as homes, families and ourselves, provide ample opportunities for displays of interesting artefacts. For example, a collection of cookery implements would provide you with the opportunity to talk with children about what they can see, encouraging them to guess what some tools might have been used for. A collection of clothing from a specific period would give them the chance to make immediate comparisons with modern dress and they could be encouraged to speculate how particular garments might have affected the behaviour and activities of the children or adults who wore them. If possible give them the opportunity to use artefacts (where appropriate) in their own activities, for example old kitchen tools during a cookery session or in the home corner or by including some simple replicas of items of period clothing in the dressing-up collection.

Since you will want the children to be able to handle objects as much as possible, do

remember when borrowing things to ask if the lender is happy with this, emphasising that the children will be encouraged to be thoughtful and careful at all times. Where a loan is made with conditions, do make sure that these are observed. If you have a local museum they might operate a loan service of artefacts suitable for young children. Remember to tell them that, wherever possible, you need objects that can be handled. Some museums might not have a loan service but will be willing to arrange for you to take the children to visit them and let them handle and talk about the artefacts there.

Evidence of change

It is not always possible to give children immediate experiences that will lead to the development of an understanding of people and places in past times. Photographs and pictures are an important resource that can be used with young children to help them consider the concepts of difference and change. Look out for and collect photographs and picture postcards of your area that illustrate how it has changed over the years. Choose two which have very clear differences - changes in shop fronts, people's dress, type or number of vehicles, buildings, and so on - and invite the children to talk about what they can see and why they think the changes might have happened.

Look at the oldest picture and talk about what it might have been like to live in the area then and how people might have felt about it. What games might the children have played? How did people do their shopping? How did children get to school?

Photographs of the children themselves as babies, as toddlers or older provide absorbing evidence of personal change. Ask parents if you can borrow some photographs of their child which show them at different stages in their lives - new-born, crawling, first birthday, walking - and let children put their photographs in chronological order and tell their story to the group or a friend. Where it is appropriate children might

attach date labels to photographs. In this way they will be introduced to the use of a time line.

Record events

Use a camera in your own setting to record different aspects of special events such as an outing and invite the children to help you to put them in the correct order in an album. Take photographs of your setting, indoors and out, which reflect seasonal changes and use these to create a book that describes key features of the children's year, for example celebrations of important festivals and their related activities such as Christmas, Chinese New Year or Eid or bare trees outside, snow on a path or playground, children wearing coats, scarves and gloves, the winter sky. Alternatively, make a book using children's drawings and paintings of such events.

Use a Polaroid camera to record the sequence followed by a group of children engaged, for example, in building with blocks or cooking. After they have finished the activity and cleared up invite them to recall the activity using the photographs and to put the photographs in the right sequence. These can then be used to create a picture book for the book area. Children will delight in revisiting these moments in their past over and over again, recalling what they did, said and felt and will find visible evidence of their own growth and change.

Stories

All children love to hear stories read and told. You can use this natural enthusiasm to introduce them to the lives of special people in the past (remember that the past doesn't have to be a long time ago, so keep an eye on the newspaper for items that will make a good story at some time). It is important to help children begin to distinguish between fiction and fact. When telling them stories, whether created in someone's imagination or about real events in the lives of real people, or a combination of fictional characters in a real historical context, tell them what sort of story they are going to hear. You could begin to make an anthology of factual historical stories that you have found the children enjoy and this will provide your setting with a useful resource in the future. Remember to update it as you tell or read new stories.

Drama

Drama is a useful tool in helping young children begin to understand that people who lived at different times were real people, that they would have had the same sort of feelings as themselves, the same desires, fears, problems and delights.

Give them opportunities to explore events in a story that they have heard and enjoyed through either self-initiated role play, role play that you have planned and structured or through an adult-directed drama session. A few well-chosen props in the role-play area will often prompt children to explore particular aspects of a story they have heard, but do remember that in self-initiated play they may choose to use the props for purposes other than those you had intended!

A well-planned drama session will allow you to build on the children's spontaneous play and more actively guide them towards thinking about particular ideas which will develop their understanding about the past and how people behaved at that time and why. It is important that you think carefully about what the children may already know from their own experience and then how you can use this to create a meaningful context which will involve them in thinking about those concepts you have selected in your planning.

Language

History starts with a child's own past and they use the knowledge about their own life history and the everyday routines that bind it together to make sense of the lives, experiences and feelings of others. It is, therefore, crucial that they are helped to develop a language that helps them to think about and describe events and people within the context of time.

(Stepping stones for a sense of time and cultures and beliefs)

Geography

Geography, like history, is about people, the places they live in, the way in which their environment affects and shapes their lives and the effects they have upon that environment through the process of living. Some of the experiences that you might provide to promote the development of children's historical understanding and skills (a visitor coming to share their memories or the use of photographs, for example) have the potential to contribute to their geographical understanding or vice-versa! It is therefore important that when you are planning activities you have a clear view of which aspect of an Early Learning Goal you are seeking to promote at any one time as a main focus (although recognising the links with other areas of learning).

Near and far

The children you work with will have a range of knowledge about a variety of places, both local and further afield, developed through either routine everyday events or special family activities. In their local area they might have walked with their parents to the local shops, visited the doctor or dentist, been to the vets, the park or playground, collected an older sibling from school and visited friends' homes. In the wider community they may have travelled by car or bus to the supermarket, the cinema, the swimming pool or been to visit relatives. Many children will also have experience of places far away from where they live as a result of going on holiday or visiting friends and relatives either in their own country or abroad and will have some understanding of long distance travel. You will need to take account of such journeys when planning your curriculum, perhaps using them as a starting point.

Journeys of discovery

Children have the ability to invest the smallest activity with the excitement of great events and journeys always have a tingle of adventure! A walk to the local shops or the park provides opportunities for children to think more carefully and deeply about well-known places as well as having fun!

If you are planning to take the children on a walk for a special purpose, do it first yourself without the children. Make sure you know about any features that you want them to notice in particular. Find out about any potential safety hazards. Be sure that the route you have planned does include the features that you want the children to think about. Brief the other adults going with you about the main focus of the activity and what to look for with the children. You might give them a map with any special features identified.

It can be helpful to bring the children together before the walk so that you can

prepare them for what they are going to be doing and why. For example, if you want them to notice particular buildings, use selected reference books to talk about the buildings in the pictures and discuss their possible use. By doing this you can be sure that every child will be able to take an active part in the walk. As they walk with you, remember that they will also want to talk about the things they see which have a special significance in their personal lives - nanny's house, the chemist's shop, the mosque, the park - as well as look for things you have identified.

Making maps

To help the children begin to understand about map-making you might take a short walk in the immediate area, choosing a route that is familiar to all the children. Before the walk, discuss with the children what they think might be the significant features of the journey, which would help to describe it to others. If possible, take a Polaroid camera with you and take pictures of these features and any others that seem significant during the walk. When you return, talk with the children about the photographs and let them choose those that they think would be the most helpful to include on a map. You could then make a simple map together with them placing the photos where they think they should go.

You can also use the photographs to stimulate the children's memories about the walk and the sequence of where things were seen, their purpose and their relationship with other buildings or objects. Both these activities would help the children acquire and use geographical language of position and location.

If you are able to obtain a blown-up aerial photograph of the area you have visited (these fascinate children) or a blown-up street map you can identify and trace the route taken with the children. Some of them might like to represent the experience by drawing a picture of things they saw on the way. A similar activity can be undertaken to represent where the children live. They can then talk about how they come to school and you can compare the different routes taken by each child. This might lead to individual map-making of these personal journeys.

Treasure hunt

Mapping activities that will involve the same skills can also be undertaken within your own setting. Help the children observe and think carefully about this part of their world that they are very familiar with and yet perhaps never really look at closely. Use games to help them begin to explore their classroom - perhaps arrange a treasure hunt with pictorial clues that will lead them to the treasure.

Organise the children into pairs so that they have the opportunity to discuss the clues and help one another. Instead of helping them with the usual hints such as 'getting warmer' or 'getting colder' you might like to give directional hints such as 'You're facing the wrong way', 'It's on your left/ alongside/in front of you' or 'You need to make a half turn'. The children can then be encouraged to draw a map of the route they took to find the treasure, which would include significant features of their classroom, and then talk about what they did with their friends. You might consider giving a child or small group the responsibility for planning such an activity including giving the verbal clues.

Language skills

There are many resources that can be used for focused work leading to the acquisition of geographical language and understanding. For example, you could give two older children an identical set of model farm animals each and a large piece of card that you have coloured to represent different fields and enclosures and with particular building features such as the farmhouse and the barn. Sit the children facing one another but put a low board or thick card partition between them so that they cannot see what each other is doing. One child then arranges their animals on the farm and then gives verbal instructions to the other child so that they produce the same arrangement. The child following the instructions should be allowed to ask questions relating to position and particular features to gain additional clarification if they need. Once finished, the two children check by comparing. The second child can then have a turn at giving the instructions and the process is repeated.

Resources such as blocks, play mats, Lego, toy cars, train sets, farms and model people offer countless opportunities for children to create real or imaginary road layouts and enact imaginary journeys. If you have a large area, indoors or outside, where the children can use wheeled toys, you might sometimes mark out a road system, in consultation with the children, so that they can re-enact journeys and explore through their imaginary play issues such as road safety. Discuss with them what road signs will be needed to ensure people's safety and let them make these.

Children also love to talk about themselves, their families and their homes. They will often draw and paint pictures of their house with family members and themselves. Could they make simple maps of areas in their own home - their bedroom perhaps? - and share and talk about these with other children? Such an activity might present an opportunity for parents to join in with their child's learning.

Sharing holiday experiences

At the end of any holiday period, but especially the summer, children are eager to share with you and their friends what they have been doing and where they have been. If possible, have large maps of the United Kingdom and the world as well as a globe (there are some inflatable plastic globes available which are light enough for young children to handle comfortably) and some copies of children's atlases.

Invite the children to bring in one photograph of their holiday that includes themselves. Discuss with them where they have been on holiday, how they travelled there, how far away it was, how long it took to get there, the relatives they visited, if any, and what they did on holiday. Help the children to locate their holiday venues on the appropriate map and/or globe and encourage them to speculate about the different places and make comparisons. If possible, display the maps on the wall with the children's photographs, or drawings they have made, and use string, wool or coloured tape to map these to the places visited. If they have any souvenirs from the countries they have visited, would they be willing to lend them for a display?

Parents from other cultures whose children attend your setting - and the children themselves - can be a rich resource. They often bring into your setting in-depth first-hand experience of other countries and ways of life that can enhance the understanding and knowledge of all the children. Perhaps a parent or grandparent could bring in a family collection of artefacts that reflect the culture and environment of their country of birth and talk about these with the children. They might be able to help a group of children cook food from their country using the appropriate cooking utensils, ingredients and processes.

People to meet

Young children are intensely curious about other people with whom they come into contact within their immediate environment. They want to know people's names and talk about the different work they see them doing, particularly when that work has some immediate impact upon the lives of themselves or other family members. Local shopkeepers or assistants, the school crossing patrol person, the local policeman or woman, the milkman, the postman or lady, the person who delivers the newspaper (the list is endless!) are all people that they will have come across and have some knowledge of before joining your group. Would any of these people be willing to come and talk to the children about what they do? Are there people within your own setting - the cook, the caretaker - who could talk to the children?

You could set up a display with a range of artefacts, including clothing, which illustrates a particular job and discuss these with the children. Alternatively, set up a display of artefacts used by people doing different jobs and encourage the children to sort them into appropriate sets, saying why they have put certain items together. Inviting other adults into your setting presents a positive opportunity to get parents involved and is often one way in which fathers and male carers are able to see that they can make a real contribution to the curriculum.

In the local area are there particular people whose work makes a unique contribution to the community, or whose work brings them into regular contact with the children, who would be willing to talk about their work? After their visit you could set up and resource a specific role-play area so that the children can explore what they have heard and seen through their imaginative play and consolidate their understanding. For example, following a visit from the district nurse, could you create a nurse's room? What might it have in it? Which patients might visit and why? A visit by a local greengrocer could lead to thinking about the different countries that fruit and vegetables come from and identifying these on the world map or globe.

Environmental issues

Our responsibility for caring for the environment is now an important issue for everyone. Introduce the children to environmental issues by giving them real opportunities to make considered choices within your setting. Involve them in discussions about the arrangement of furniture and resources in the classroom. Are things in the right place for the work you all want or need to do? Remind them that they will need to consider not only their own needs but also those of friends and the adults who support them.

Talk with them about how you might develop the outdoor area. What sort of features might be included? Could you develop a simple conservation area where grass and wild flowers could grow unchecked and insects are encouraged to visit or live? Could they help to design the area? What sort of impact might this have on their usual outdoor activities and on their own behaviour? How might they resolve this conflict of need?

Talk about the local area with them and the sort of things they like to do there. How well does the local area meet their needs? Go for a walk and look for good and bad features in the context of their needs.

On their return let them draw designs or build a three-dimensional map of how they think the area could look. Remind them of their shared responsibility for the immediate environment - tidying up and returning things they have used in their play to their proper place is a first step into beginning to take responsibility for the wider environment we all inhabit.

(Stepping stones for a sense of place, and cultures and beliefs)

More detailed support to assist practitioners is provided in the 'Examples of what children do' and 'What does the practitioner need to do?' sections that accompany each of the Foundation Stage goals, including the Early Learning Goals.

Physical
Development

There is no significant difference between the DLOs and the Early Learning Goals except that the different elements have been separated and the aspect of 'health and bodily awareness' has been expanded for greater clarity.

There are eight Early Learning Goals for this area of learning and these are divided into five categories.

Early Learning Goals for movement
- Move with confidence, imagination and in safety

- Move with control and coordination

- Travel around, under, over and through balancing and climbing equipment

22 stepping stones including the above ELGs

Early Learning Goals for sense of space
- Show awareness of space, of themselves and of others

8 stepping stones including the above ELG

Early Learning Goals for health and bodily awareness
- Recognise the importance of keeping healthy and those things which contribute to this

- Recognise the changes that happen to their bodies when they are active

7 stepping stones including the above ELGs

Early Learning Goals for using equipment
- Use a range of small and large equipment

6 stepping stones including the above ELG

Early Learning Goals for using tools and materials

- Handle tools, objects, construction and malleable materials safely and with increasing control

10 stepping stones including the above ELG

Achievement of these stepping stones, including the Early Learning Goals, will occur across the Foundation Stage curriculum as well as in specifically planned activities that have a particular focus relating to an aspect of this area of learning.

'Physical Development in the Foundation Stage is about improving skills of coordination, control, manipulation and movement. ... It helps children gain confidence in what they can do and enables them to feel the positive benefits of being healthy and active.'

Young children's physical development contributes to all other aspects of their development. It is about large and fine motor activity - running, walking, jumping, climbing and dancing as well as cutting, drawing, painting, writing or gluing.

Sense of self
When playing on a climbing frame, slide or with wheeled toys children can learn and practise a variety of skills. They develop their personal and social skills as they learn to wait and take turns and consider other's feelings. They develop their language skills as they negotiate who should go first, listen to each other or decide what should

happen next. Mathematical skills are used as they look and count how many bikes there are or match them to the children there to see if there are enough. They use the language of position, which relates to both mathematics and reading, to describe their movements as they climb on the climbing frame. As they play on the see-saw or rocking horse they begin to think about weight and balance and the relationship between them. Outdoors they explore the world around them and wonder at its many marvels. As they ride bikes and scooters or push a pram they experience different speeds and relate these to their effort and energy. Above all they develop a holistic sense of self - an awareness of the shape and movements of their bodies, the spaces and other people around them and how they relate to them as they move - and their feelings of self-esteem and self-worth are fostered. They learn about themselves. That is why you should ensure that the children have sustained opportunities, preferably every day, for all aspects of their physical development when you plan your programme.

The importance of outdoor play

Young children need to be able to move vigorously and freely - it is part of their natural development. They also need to be able to make choices, follow interests and exercise their growing independence. That is why purpose-built early years provision is normally designed to include a safe and secure outdoor play space where children can spontaneously develop their physical skills as they play. In this space children can move freely without worrying about bumping into objects and can exercise their voices without being told that they are being too noisy! No matter how generous your hall or room spaces the children cannot move and play as they do outdoors. They cannot exercise in the way that they do outdoors. Outside they are subject to the effects of weather - sunshine and cold - that affects the body's movements and they learn to make adjustments. They can feel what it is like to be part of a much larger space than that indoors - where walls, ceilings and furniture constrain movement - and begin to experience the immensity of the natural world and their place in it.

This sort of physical activity and play is of special importance today because many parents feel unable to let their children play outdoors, even in the garden, because of fears for their safety. Many children live in flats or maisonettes and do not have access to a garden area unless they are taken there. The place of physical activity and exercise is therefore vital in the early years curriculum if all children are to develop as healthy and happy individuals.

If your provision has its own outdoor space then you need to think how you are going to incorporate this space into your daily planning. What sort of activities will you make available to challenge every aspect of the children's physical development? How can you make sure that they have easy access to this area for most of each session and how will the adults interact with and contribute to the children's play? If you don't have immediate access to this area from your room you will need to work out how children can use the outdoor space as much as possible.

Finding alternatives

If you do not have an outdoor area you will need to think about how to overcome this. Is there a local nursery or primary school that would let you use some or all of their outdoor play area? Is there a parent with a reasonably large garden who might let you use this with either all or some of the children on a regular basis? What equipment will you need to take with you - for example, a first aid kit? Make sure that the place you choose is within reasonable walking distance for young children and that you have enough adults to supervise

the children safely as they walk. If none of these options are possible then you could build into your programme regular opportunities for the children to go for short walks, perhaps to a local park or green space where they can move freely and spontaneously. This is particularly important today since many families rely upon the car for most of their journeys and many young children have too few opportunities to develop a healthy lifestyle.

Useful tip for safer walks

A useful aid when taking even a group of very young children out for a walk is a length of strong rope that has shorter lengths knotted across at regular intervals. With an adult holding each end the children then walk either side of the rope holding onto the cross-pieces. The rope gives the children a clear visual signal of what they are expected to do, they feel safe and secure and the adults supervising can see each child easily since they are spaced out along the rope.

Adapting space indoors

Does your provision have a reasonably large indoor space, without furniture, that you could use in addition to the classroom? If so, it might be worth thinking about letting the children use this space more often for spontaneous play. Although it cannot offer the same challenge as that outside, the extra space will allow them to incorporate larger physical movement into their play. You will need to plan which activities and resources you could move into this space to encourage the children to incorporate large movement in their play without being directed. For example, could you put a tape recorder and tapes of different types of music and/or some musical instruments in one corner along with some dressing-up/dance clothing so that children are encouraged to make up their own dances? A display of photographs of people dancing may act as a further stimulus.

(Stepping stones for movement)

Organising space outside

If you do have an outdoor area, take a long hard look at it. Is it attractive and interesting? Just as you organise your indoor environment into clearly defined spaces so that children can make sense of it, so you need to do the same with your outdoor area.

- Are there larger spaces where the children can ride wheeled toys, run and move about freely and safely or play with small games equipment such as balls?

- Are there smaller spaces where children can role-play?

- Is there a space where they can write, draw or paint if they want to?

- If you have slides and swings is there a clear space around them?

- Are there tree trunks on which children can climb and balance or which they can jump on and off?

- Can the children move indoor activities and resources outside as they need?

- In planning your curriculum do you plan for both the inside and outside spaces as one area?

There are many ways to provide focused activities outside that parallel those inside and challenge children's large and fine motor skills. For example, painting easels inside can be complemented with painting outside on large sheets of paper and using large decorating brushes. Clay and dough can be taken outside as well as used indoors. You might feel that some activities such as woodwork are better outdoors, when the weather makes this possible, because of the noise! Indoors, children can fill and empty using small containers and plastic tubing in the weather tray. Outside they can use buckets and pieces of guttering and drainpipe. Planting bulbs or cress inside can be complemented with gardening outside and learning how to use spades, forks and trowels that are appropriately sized. Remember that if children are to learn successfully they need equipment that works and know how to use it safely. You can even take children outside for planned gymnastics, dance or games lessons for most of the year, although you might want to make sessions shorter during the winter months. It is often easier to play with equipment such as balls outside where there is less danger of causing damage!

(*Stepping stones for movement, sense of space, using equipment and using tools and materials*)

Planned activities

As well as the spontaneous opportunities for physical development provided in the indoor and outdoor environment you will also want to provide planned opportunities specifically to develop the children's physical skills and abilities, particularly those related to dance, gymnastics and games. It is important to remember when planning any focused games, dance or gymnastics sessions that such activity is probably well outside many young children's experience, as is working and responding to precise adult instructions, either yours or those accompanying a music and movement tape. They may well be unused to working in a large hall or outside play area. For some children, getting undressed or changing into other clothing can be daunting. You will therefore need to be sensitive to the different needs of the children and give them time to become accustomed to these new demands.

Keep it simple

Children need to enjoy the experiences you offer and so you should build on what the children are already familiar with when planning activities. Many of them will be familiar with simple songs and action rhymes and you will be extending this repertoire daily. Rather than launching into separate gymnastics, dance or games lessons, which may well require the children to use skills they have not yet developed, start with what they can do. Choose a

known action rhyme into which you can incorporate movement that the children can do - running, walking, galloping, hopping, skipping - and let them move to this while you all say the rhyme together. They will be able to concentrate on and respond to your instructions - for example, stop, start and change - more easily since they do not have to think about other things.

Introduce the words associated with different parts of the body and actions during this period and begin to encourage them to think more carefully about their own movements - running softly on their toes, creeping quietly like a cat, or making themselves tall as a giraffe by stretching up as they walk. As they become more confident, introduce a different but familiar stimulus. Well-known stories often lend themselves to movement/dance interpretation. Perhaps having read one at story time you could talk to the children about how the story might be interpreted in this way. Remember to set realistic targets that build on and extend those loco-motor skills you have been working on already. Only when the children are secure and confident in the space you use and can respond to your instructions should you think about using percussion instruments or taped music, particularly if the tape also gives movement instructions for the children to follow. These early lessons will also provide a starting point for the separate elements of games and gymnastics.

Games to play

The children will already know about playing some games from home. At this age the emphasis should not be upon competition but rather upon enjoyment. At first choose games that do not need any equipment but give further practice in responding to signals and becoming more aware of spatial language - up, down, under, on, over, high, low, and so on. Most children enjoy playing games such as 'Simon Says', 'Statues' or 'Grandmother's Footsteps'. There are many others that help them to learn spatial language, the names of body parts, and to respond to instructions. Introduce equipment such as balls, hoops, quoits and beanbags gradually and only when the children are confident about using the space. Give them plenty of opportunities to experiment with each type of equipment. Young children need time and practice in order to develop their skills.

Large apparatus

If you have a climbing frame, slide, tunnels and other agility equipment such as swing bridges outside children will readily choose to play on these often incorporating elements into their imaginative play - the climbing frame can wonderfully represent a building where a group of firefighters clamber up, down, over and through as they put out a fire.

Don't be tempted to use large fixed indoor gymnastic apparatus too soon. Give children time to explore and begin to control and co-ordinate their own body movements first. Learning how to balance yourself is hard enough on the floor without adding the further difficulty of doing this on a raised bar or plank! Always let the children practise their movements on the floor before asking them to transfer these to apparatus. When you feel that the children are ready to use the large apparatus, only use that which will support your learning objectives. For example, if your objective is to help the children to develop their balancing skills you may only need one or two benches.

You may feel that getting out any apparatus halfway through a session is not possible with young children because of the difficulties of supervision. This should not be seen as a problem since from the beginning you should be training them to handle and move apparatus. This might mean that in the early stages you feel that they take so long getting the apparatus out that there is little time to actually use it! Be patient and remember that they will only get better through practice!

(Stepping stones for movement, sense of space)

In all their physical activity, whether spontaneous or in response to a planned activity, encourage the children to think about what their bodies are doing as a result of their exertions. For example, children will often say, 'I'm sweating' after they have been running around or will describe feelings of dizziness after twirling round and round or say, 'My heart's thumping'. Use such opportunities to talk with the children about exercise and its effect upon their health as well as inviting them to speculate upon why these things are happening.

(Stepping stones for movement, sense of space, using equipment and health and bodily awareness)

Your role

In all the physical development activities that you provide for the children, both spontaneous and focused, it is important to think about your role. What sort of interactions will help and encourage them to begin to consider the movements more carefully? How can you balance praise with comments that will provide an appropriate challenge to improve? Remember that the conversations you have with the children, and the comments and questions you ask as part of this, play a significant part in ensuring that they develop all their physical skills, as they should.

More detailed support to assist practitioners is provided in the 'Examples of what children do' and 'What does the practitioner need to do?' sections that accompany each of the Foundation Stage goals, including the Early Learning Goals.

Stories as starters

If you want to use a stimulus to help children think about their movements, one good idea is to use a story. There are many to choose from that would work well. For example, *Rosie's Walk* by Pat Hutchins tells the story of Rosie the hen who, while out for a walk around the farmyard is followed by a hungry fox with alternative plans for her! The story is full of gentle humour much appreciated by young children. You might try recreating the story events using simple apparatus such as benches and hoops. As you tell the story, the children can do Rosie's actions - under the fence means they have to crawl or wriggle under a bench, round the duck pond means stepping carefully around a hoop, and so on.

Creative Development

There is little difference between the content of the DLOs and the Early Learning Goals. However, for the purposes of clarity of both reading and understanding some have been reworded and/or expanded.

There are five Early Learning Goals for this area of learning and these are divided into four categories.

Early Learning Goals for exploring media and materials

● Explore colour, texture, shape, form and space in two or three dimensions

15 stepping stones including the above ELG

Early Learning Goals for music

● Recognise and explore how sounds can be changed, sing simple songs from memory, recognise repeated sounds and sound patterns and match movements to music

13 stepping stones including the above ELG

Early Learning Goals for imagination

● Use their imagination in art and design, music, dance, imaginative and role play and stories

11 stepping stones including the above ELG

Early Learning Goals for responding to experiences, and expressing and communicating ideas

● Respond in a variety of ways to what they see, hear, smell, touch and feel

● Express and communicate their ideas, thoughts and feelings by using a widening range of materials, suitable tools, imaginative and role play, movement, designing and making, and a variety of songs and musical instruments

12 stepping stones including the above ELGs

Achievement of these stepping stones, including the Early Learning Goals, will occur across the Foundation Stage curriculum as well as in specifically planned activities that have a particular focus relating to an aspect of this area of learning.

Being creative is all about being able to use past experiences and rearrange or transform them to make and communicate new ideas. It means being able to respond to the world around us emotionally, using all the senses. It is about making believe, imagining the 'What if ...?', being willing to put oneself in other people's shoes and consider different ideas. It is about taking risks!

Future societies will need people who can develop novel solutions to all sorts of problems. Those who have been supported to develop as creative and divergent thinkers from early childhood will be better able to respond to those challenges.

Dramatic play

As young children play out different roles - being a mum or dad, a firefighter, a dog - and recreate some event - looking after the children, putting out a fire - they transform themselves and objects through their imaginations. The beads become a bowl of food to be fed to the 'baby'; the skipping rope becomes a hose gushing out water. What they do not know about putting out a fire they make up from other experiences that, to them, seem similar! As they play with toy boats in the water they meet storms at sea and imagine dangers. As they play with the train set they feel the power and the responsibility of driving the train. As they drive the cars on the road built with blocks they deal with all the responsibilities of being a driver.

In their spontaneous play anything is possible; risks can be taken because they are in control and problems can be solved through the imagination.

Spontaneous play

All young children need help to be creative and imaginative. It is therefore important that they have substantial time each day when they can choose what they want to do and work through their ideas in their play. This spontaneous play is of the utmost importance since it gives them the freedom to explore their own ideas in their own way. In planning your curriculum you will need to be flexible whilst also maintaining a balance between spontaneous play and those focused or structured play activities which you have set up to introduce particular ideas. You will need to look at your environment both inside and outside.

● Does it help the children to develop their own play?

● Is there enough floor space for large constructions?

- Does the home corner have enough space for children to really explore roles?

- Do the experiences on offer outside complement those inside whilst reflecting the particular nature of either the outdoors or indoors - for example, a sand tray indoors and a digging area outside, a home corner indoors and materials for making a den outdoors?

- Can children move around easily from one space to another?

- Are there things for children to play with which are open-ended and so allow them to use their imagination?

- Do you have sets of different sized blocks, clay, dough, dressing-up clothes, dolls and so on?

- Do you allow them to use resources from one area in another - for example, can

they use the counting cubes to represent food in the home corner (as long as they put things back in the right place when clearing up)?

It is sometimes useful to build up random collections of objects - shells, pebbles, fir cones, buttons, model people and animals, ribbons, bits left from withdrawn resources such as jigsaw pieces - which the children know they can use in any way, which will help to preserve more precious and expensive resources. The children might contribute to these collections by bringing in old toys from home.

You will also need to think about how you are going to support the children in their spontaneous play. You will need to observe

play activity if you are to intervene and support the children effectively.

- What ideas are they exploring and trying to make sense of?

- How can you help them sort out their ideas?

Without observation there is always the danger that you can misunderstand what the play is about and offer the wrong information or substitute your own ideas for theirs thus devaluing their creativity.

- When they share their ideas with you, how will you show them that you consider these to be of real importance?

The role of stories

If children are to play imaginatively they need a rich diet of experiences to feed their imagination. The richer the range of experiences from which the children can select the greater their opportunity to explore the things that interest them and develop new ideas.

Literature has a special contribution to make. Through story children can encounter people they may never meet, visit places they may never go to, witness events they may never see and worlds and times they may never live in. They can then choose from and transform this material as they create a story script for their own play - Superman meets Cinderella!

Some stories demonstrate how elements from one story can be transformed into a new story with surprising results. Alan Ahlberg's *The Jolly Postman* is one such example. Reading and talking about stories like this to children tells them that using your imagination to transform elements into something new and exciting is not only acceptable but also fun!

(Stepping stones for imagination)

Art and craft

Young children are continually reacting to, transforming and representing the world around them through play. Many of the experiences that you provide across the curriculum have the potential to contribute to children's aesthetic and creative development. However, there are particular experiences that make a special contribution to this aspect of the curriculum - art, craft, music, drama and dance - and it is these aspects that you will need to consider when planning your curriculum. (Dance is dealt with on pages 30-31 under Physical Development. However, there will be a need to consider the Early Learning Goals relating to music, the imagination and responding to experiences, expressing ideas and emotions, as well as those for Physical Development when children are engaged in spontaneous or planned movement/dance activities.)

Art and craft includes painting, drawing, printing, collage, sewing, woodwork, sculpture and pottery. Some of these will result in two-dimensional work whilst others will lead to working in three dimensions.

Being creative means developing, representing and communicating your own ideas and experiences in your own way so it is important that children are allowed to do exactly that. Filling in someone else's drawing with tissue paper, fabric or paint, drawing round templates, colouring in pre-drawn shapes, tracing and sticking pre-cut shapes to reproduce an adult's model pattern do not challenge children to think for themselves nor allow them to represent their ideas. As important is the damage that can be done to young children's self-esteem from the implicit message of such activities - that their ideas are of no value and their skills ineffectual. In other words, there is a right way and a wrong way - and they get it wrong!

To become skilful with different materials young children need time to explore them and to find out what each can and can't do. It is only through such initial exploration

'Creativity is fundamental to successful learning. Being creative enables children to make connections between one area of learning and another and so extend their learning.'

that they will be able to make a considered choice about which material will best represent an idea or experience.

If children are to learn about and understand the properties of different materials then they need to have regular access to them and time to test out and consolidate their learning. Having access to clay on an occasional basis does not help children to develop an understanding of what clay might be most suitable for as a means of communication and how to work with it effectively.

This means that you will need to consider carefully the variety of materials that you can make available.

● Is there an area where children know there is a variety of mark-making tools - pencils, crayons, coloured pencils, felt-tip pens, chalk, charcoal and a range of paper (white is best) of different sizes - where they can draw?

● Are the pencils of differing quality not just HB? 2B and 3B pencils have quite different properties - they can be smudged and lines can be blended - and so offer different possibilities.

● Is the paper you provide of good quality, capable of taking marks and properly cut? It is hard for children to take care in their drawing and do their best when the quality of the materials say that this is not an important activity or where poor quality prevents them from realising their ideas.

● Is there a computer that they can use with an appropriate software package to explore computer imagery?

● Is there a printer so that they can print out their finished work?

● Is there an area where children can mix their own colours when painting so that they can better recreate experiences and are there ready-mixed paints for those children who need to paint quickly in order to capture a personal event?

● Is there a range of brushes available - pointed, straight, bristle, sable - in different sizes, to suit the variety of painting tasks that the children might want to undertake?

● Are there opportunities to add other materials to paint - sand, glue, and cornflour - to recreate texture?

● Is there an area where they can create three dimensionally, selecting from a range of materials - wood, soap bars, salt blocks, clay, dough, wet sand, reclaimed materials - and a range of tools and materials for joining and fastening that they can use to manipulate these materials?

● Is there an area where they can use fabrics and threads with sharp scissors that will cut?

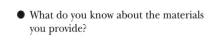

● What do you know about the materials you provide?

● How do they behave when they are handled?

● What are their constraints and their strengths - what works and what doesn't in particular circumstances?

Explore together each of the materials you provide one by one, then share your experiences.

● What skills did you need? Which tools were helpful and which weren't?

● What did you find frustrating? How did the material feel? What worked and why?

By doing this you will be better able to talk to the children about their experiences, teach appropriate skills as they are needed, provide appropriate and interesting vocabulary and help them to develop and refine their representations.

Children need to be presented with a range of experiences that will stimulate them to try out all these materials and arouse their imagination. Very young children can be introduced to the work of artists and craftspeople, both 2-d and 3-d, to enhance their knowledge about arts and crafts. Encourage them to talk about what they see, the use of colour, line, pattern and texture, how it makes them feel and what they think the person who created the painting or object was trying to say. Share your own ideas and feelings with the children. Looking at and talking about works of art provides them with a more extensive repertoire of what they might be able to do.

Can you involve a practising artist in your setting? (If there is an art group in your area this could be your first point of contact.) They could show the children a sketchbook diary in which they quickly record things that they have seen or explain how they select an image and compose a picture. Would they be prepared to come in sometimes as the children are working and talk to those painting, drawing or modelling about their work? If this is possible, bear in mind that they may need help when talking to young children.

The displays in your environment will also foster children's imaginative responses to the world about them. If you can't mount displays on walls perhaps you can set up small 3-d displays of objects which have interesting shapes, textures or colours which can be put away at the end of sessions. If you do mount displays, make sure that they don't become like wallpaper - they are there to stimulate the children's aesthetic and creative sensibilities. It is far better to have less of high quality than so much that it is impossible to really see anything at all.

(Stepping stones for exploring media and materials, for imagination and for responding to experiences, and expressing and communicating ideas)

Music

Most young children have a substantial musical repertoire before they attend an early years setting. Music accompanies adverts on television, is used to create mood in television programmes, and is played in shops and stores as background music. Children may have family members who enjoy listening to music or who are musicians. Many will have tapes of songs and rhymes that they listen to regularly.

It is likely that many of them will have memories of being sung to. It is not unusual to hear children singing to themselves. They will often sing the jingles that accompany well-known adverts and make up their own words to known tunes.

They delight in exploring sound! The early years setting needs to build on and extend these early experiences.

● Is there an area in your setting where children have regular access to a range of musical instruments and where they can explore sound patterns and make music spontaneously? Consider carefully where to position such an area since it can be noisy!

● Are there planned opportunities when they can come together to make music using untuned percussion instruments? Can the children make a collection of objects from your environment that make interesting sounds or even make their own instruments?

● Do you help them to understand and appreciate musical stories by providing opportunities for them to 'tell' a well-liked and familiar story using sounds instead of words? Encourage them to think how they might represent characters and events in the story with sounds. What sort of sounds would best describe the giant in 'Jack and the Beanstalk', for example, and how might these change when he's asleep?

● Can they write down their compositions so that they can be replayed? Instead of using conventional notation encourage them to listen carefully to each sound they make and then create a descriptive symbol to represent it. A crash on the cymbal might look like a spiral; a zigzag could be repetitive taps on a drum.

● Can you set up a quiet listening area where they can choose to listen to short pieces of carefully chosen music, representing a variety of styles, on tape?

Provide planned opportunities when they can come together to listen to a piece of music; help them to listen carefully and talk about how the music made them feel and what it made them think of. Demonstrate the importance of the activity by sharing your own feelings and ideas created by the music at the end. Perhaps you could build up your own collection of musical pieces that you all like.

Most children love to sing and make sound. Help them to learn a range of simple songs and rhymes and provide them with opportunities to sing together. If you can't play the piano to accompany them don't worry, they will enjoy having you sing along with them.

If singing yourself worries you, see if you can get a pianist friend to tape record the piano accompaniment to favourite songs that you can use with the children during singing. If you do this, invite the pianist in to listen to the children singing before making the tape so that they are aware of what is needed. As well as singing, help the children to develop their awareness of rhythm, pace and pulse by teaching them rhythmic chants or by using repetitive refrains from familiar stories such as 'The Gingerbread Man'.

Bring in people from your community or professional musicians who can perform to the children or who might be willing to work with the children as they make and create music.

(Stepping stones for music, for imagination and for responding to experiences and expressing and communicating ideas)

> **More detailed support to assist practitioners is provided in the 'Examples of what children do' and 'What does the practitioner need to do?' sections that accompany each of the Foundation Stage goals, including the Early Learning Goals.**

Assessment and record-keeping

Within the curriculum the following feature of good practice should be present - 'identification of the progress and future learning needs of children through observations which are evaluated, recorded and shared regularly with parents, so that each child's particular needs are met'.

Part of the inspection process undertaken by Ofsted includes looking at and evaluating how a setting assesses children's attainment and progress. Inspectors look at how the adults working with the children make assessments of children and how information about children is recorded. They look, too, at how the adults use this information to plan future work for children that will match individual needs. Such matching ensures that children can make progress towards the Early Learning Goals and the early stages of the National Curriculum Programmes of Study for English and mathematics. Inspectors also consider how the staff monitor and assess the curriculum and their own teaching so that they can maintain and develop practice of high quality.

Building up a picture

Adults who spend time with children, listening to their ideas about what they are doing, the world they know and the people in it, having conversations with them about those ideas and watching what they do, cannot help but begin to know more about, and make judgements about, those children. They begin to build up a picture or profile of each child. These profiles may include such things as what interests particular children, the things they know, favourite toys and activities, who is best friends with whom - and who isn't, how they tackle activities and what they do when things don't work out as they had anticipated. The list is endless! Very often what is learned about children on these occasions is informal and unplanned but the information gained helps to build up a picture that influences the way that the adults will respond to those children in the future.

Asking parents for information

Most settings have a registration form that is completed with parents before children begin attendance. This usually asks for information such as family details, emergency contacts, and important information about a child such as allergies, particular physical needs, food likes and dislikes and information about any previous childcare. It is worth thinking about whether there is other information that you might ask for, in addition to these more administrative details. Parents have been informally observing their children since they were born and know a great deal about them. For example, does a child have particular things he or she likes to do, such

as building with Lego or making believe? Do they like to hear stories and have particular favourites? What sorts of things worry or upset them? How do parents deal with misbehaviour? Knowing this sort of information will help you better plan for the children when they start attending and form a first profile to which you and they can begin to add.

From the day that children begin in a setting, good early childhood workers begin to collect information that will help them to provide the best care and education for each child. However, it is important to remember that when a child first starts in your setting there will be many unfamiliar things happening and different routines and people for them to get to know. Therefore some of the behaviour that you note during the first few weeks may not give you a true picture of the child. Further observations will enable you to decide whether the judgements you have made about each child during these early weeks require modification, or may continue to form the basis for your response to their needs.

Home visits

Some settings undertake home visiting, provided that the parents are happy for the staff to visit them in their homes. Home visiting gives staff the chance to see the child in their own home where they are secure and confident. Some staff allow time for talking and playing with the child during the visit and make a simple record of what they have observed. Parents are always interested in their children and if you share this first recorded observation with them it will encourage them to want to share in the process and make their own contributions both during the visit and in the future. This collaboration between yourselves and parents will ensure that you develop a rounded picture for each of the children in your care. Therefore whilst home visiting can require careful organisation and take time, those settings who undertake this find that it is a worthwhile and valuable activity.

Observing children

Early years settings are normally busy and lively places with children involved in a wide variety of activities and where adults are fully occupied supporting them. As the adults interact with the children they are noticing what they are doing and how they are coping and tailor how they respond to them in the light of these observations. Often they make mental notes about what they have observed rather than writing things down. Because of the nature of any early years setting there is no way that the staff can be alongside each child all the time. Therefore the incidental observations, from which assessments may be made, may not always give a full picture of every child. Observation - watching and listening - is a key skill that practitioners need to develop.

doing across the whole curriculum. For this reason it is important to make systematic and planned observations of each child to accompany those that occur incidentally. In this way you will be able to build up a profile of their development in all its aspects.

Recording on the spot

There are times when you may want to record an incidental observation you make quickly, perhaps something you have seen a child do, or something they say, that you feel is significant and that you don't want to

statement at the front of the book. If there is a note that has information that you think you want to keep stick this one next to your written summary, otherwise throw them away. This can be a useful way of monitoring whether some children are being overlooked by staff since these children will have no notes stuck in their books. As you are checking on a weekly basis, you can make sure that the adults in your setting make a particular effort to look out for these children in the following week.

Think carefully about your children and any informal observations you have recorded. You may find that for some children you have several recorded observations whilst for others you have very few. There are always some children that, for a variety of reasons, take up a great deal of adult time! There are always some children who, perhaps because they are quiet or well behaved, receive less adult time. Equally you may find that whilst you have recorded some observations of a child they tend to be very similar. They do not give you a picture of what that child is

forget. One way of dealing with such occasions is to use self-stick notes (you will also need a board or door that you can use to stick the notes to and a small exercise book for each child). Jot down only the essential details on the self-stick note, including the child's name and date, and then stick it on the board/door. At the end of the session collect up the notes that you and others may have completed and then re-stick them on a back page of the appropriate child's exercise book. At the end of each week, sort through the notes in each child's book and write a summary

The children will be fascinated by the notes stuck up on the board and will want to know what you have written. Don't be afraid to tell them! You will find that sharing your observations with them will help them both to talk about their activity and learning with you and begin to evaluate their own progress. The process will fascinate parents too, once you have explained what you are doing and why, and the notes will provide an opportunity for them to become part of your observation, assessment and record-keeping process. It may even prompt parents to share observations they have made of their children's behaviour at home that they had not previously thought of as important.

Written records
Whilst it may not be necessary to record all the daily incidental observations you make of children, it is important to record any specific planned observations that you make. Having a written record of what actually happened will enable you to reflect on what a child was doing and help you to make a more careful assessment of their understanding. If you work within a team, share your observations and decide together what you need to do next for that particular child. There are no right ways to record children's progress. However, it is important to keep paperwork to manageable proportions!

Formal assessment
In order to make formal assessments you will need to know what you are going to assess. First, you need to look carefully at your long-term planned curriculum to make sure that the planned learning leads towards achievement in all of the Early Learning Goals. For example, do all the children have spontaneous and planned opportunities to use and enjoy books, recognise and write their own names and take part in role play? Do they have opportunities to make mathematical patterns and learn number rhymes and songs? Does your programme provide them with opportunities to explore features of living things or to talk about past and present events in their lives? Do they have opportunities to co-operate with others through working in small groups and respond to cultural and religious events? You will also want to look at how you intend to provide these opportunities - what will the children be doing? Are there some regular routines that will provide you with assessment opportunities, such as changing for physical activities, listening to stories or snack-times?

Identifying learning targets
Whilst you will be undertaking both informal and formal observations on a regular basis it is

useful to look at your long- and medium-term planning and identify key points for assessment. In this way you can ensure that you are observing children and the progress they are making towards the Early Learning Goals.

You may use termly or half-termly themes to introduce and teach certain aspects of areas of learning and these will undoubtedly present observation and assessment opportunities. Your weekly and daily planning should contain more detailed information about assessment opportunities - the activity itself, which child or children is/are going to be formally observed, where this will take place, the time it will be done and for how long and who will be doing it. Most important of all is to identify what the intended learning target is, for example holding a pencil correctly, cutting round an outline with a pair of scissors, recognising their name or mathematical shapes, solving a problem or sharing with others. You may find the stepping stones contained in the *Curriculum Guidance* useful in determining which targets to set. Whatever the agreed target is it should be included in your

planning so that everyone knows what the focus is for the selected children.

By making observation and assessment part of your short-term planning you should find that you are able to manage it more effectively so that it does not become a burden. There should be no need to create special activities to undertake the assessments that you want to make. Indeed, to do so could often be counter productive since the children may well feel insecure and therefore less confident doing something that is not a regular and normal part of their programme. Instead you will need to think carefully about the activities you are providing and consider what assessment opportunities they present.

Focus on individuals
You will want to be sure that all the children are regularly observed and assessed. In addition to any focused individual or group assessment activities that you have planned it is useful to identify one or two children each day for general observation. Ask any staff working with you to note down what either the child or children do and their achievements on any occasions that they come in contact with them. At the end of the session or day, find time to talk together about what has been observed and come to an agreement about progress. These comments can be added to the appropriate profiles.

Collecting evidence
There are a variety of ways to gather information about children in addition to jottings of incidental observations and records of formal observations. Photographs are useful for recording such things as constructions that children have made with blocks but which cannot be kept. Tape recordings can be made of children talking - children love to hear themselves! Collections can be made of samples of children's work across the curriculum. It is up to the staff in each setting to decide what is appropriate for them and the children who attend.

Whilst observation, assessment and record keeping together represent a complex and demanding process they are essential activities in ensuring that early education is meeting the varied and individual needs of all the children and is providing high quality experiences that challenge and extend them all.

	Week 1	Week 2	Week 3	Week 4	Week 5	Week 6
Child's name				Date of Birth		Term
Personal, Social and Emotional Development						
Communication, Language and Literacy						
Mathematical Development						
Knowledge and Understanding of the World						
Physical Development						
Creative Development						